A COMPLETE MATHS PROGRAM FOR PRIMARY SCHOOLS

Planet Maths

1st Class

GW00808507

Proinsias Ó Conghaile agus Elaine McCann

FOLENS

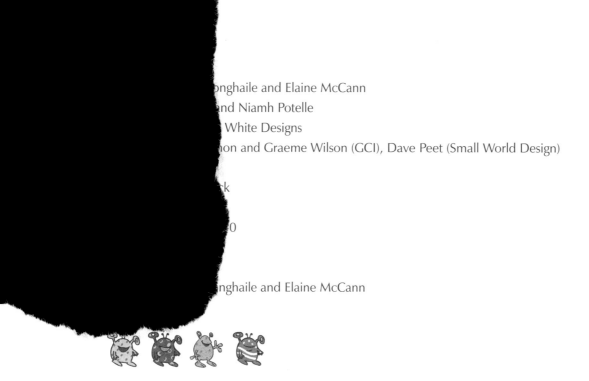

onghaile and Elaine McCann

nd Niamh Potelle

White Designs

on and Graeme Wilson (GCI), Dave Peet (Small World Design)

k

0

nghaile and Elaine McCann

First published in 2011 by: Folens Publishers,
Hibernian Industrial Estate, Greenhills Road, Tallaght, Dublin 24.
Produced in Ireland by Folens Publishers.

The paper used in this book is sourced from managed forests.

Introduction for Parents and Teachers

Planet Maths has been developed by a team of experienced primary teachers and Maths consultants in accordance with the aims and objectives of the revised Primary School Curriculum and the accompanying Teacher Guidelines. Curriculum Strands, Strand Units and Objectives are detailed throughout.

The series underpins the key areas of:

- Use of concrete materials
- Development and correct use of mathematical language
- Real life problem solving
- Cooperative group work
- Oral maths
- Estimation
- Written computation
- Integration with other subjects

Planet Maths is a creative new maths series that aims to provide children with challenging activities and enjoyable mathematical experiences to help them become confident mathematicians.

Poster pages

The purpose of the five double-page Poster Pages in the book is to introduce or revise a strand or strand unit(s) through talk and discussion. More formal engagement with the strand or strand unit(s) will follow at a later stage.

For ease of use, the **Maths Curriculum strands** are colour coded as follows:

Multiple	TEAL		**Shape and Space**	PURPLE
Measures	GREEN		**Data**	RED
Number	BLUE		**Algebra**	ORANGE

The **Teacher's Manual** accompanying this textbook includes:

- A guide providing comprehensive suggestions on how to make the best use of this series;
- Oral and mental maths activity suggestions;
- Maths language relevant to each topic;
- Suggestions for using concrete materials and manipulatives;
- Photocopiable activities for differentiation and extension exercises;
- Photocopiable templates for practice and repetition of fundamental concepts;
- Answers;
- Assessment sheets;
- Individual student profile sheets;
- Class record sheets.

Interactive activities for this series can also be found at *www.folensonline.ie*.

Authors

Rita Coleman and Liam Gaynor (6th), Elaine Burke (5th), Liam Gaynor (4th), Sue-Anne Synnott (3rd), Veronica Hande and Veronica Ward (2nd), Proinsias Ó Conghaile and Elaine McCann (1st), Angela Curley (Senior Infants), Deirdre Whelan (Junior Infants)

Contents

I am looking back at what I did in Senior Infants.

A Warm-up. Listen to your teacher. Use your counters.

| 1 | 2 | 3 | 4 | 5 | 6 | 7 | 8 | 9 |

B Count and colour.

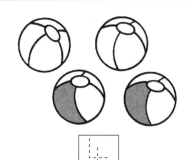 4

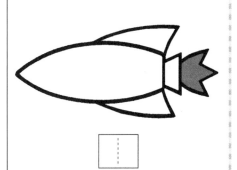 1

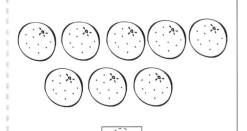 8

 2

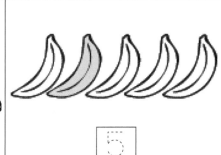 5

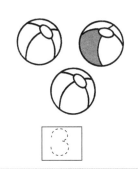 3

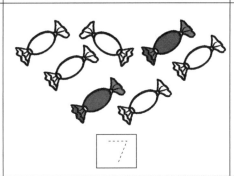 7

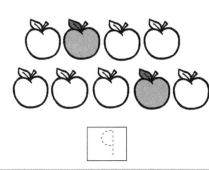 9

C How many?

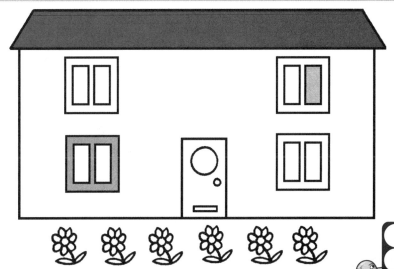

Revision

A Write the numbers.

1 2 3 4 5 6 7 8 9

B Fill in the missing numbers.

1 one	2 two	3 three	4 four	5 five	6 six	7 seven	8 eight	9 nine

1	2		4		6	7		
	2	3			6			
1				5				9
			4				8	

C Write the words.

1 _____one_____

2 _____

3 _____

4 _____

5 _____

6 _____

7 _____

8 _____

9 _____

D Join the dots. Colour.

A Colour only 5 stars.

B Colour the picture.   How many?

Colour the correct number of blocks.

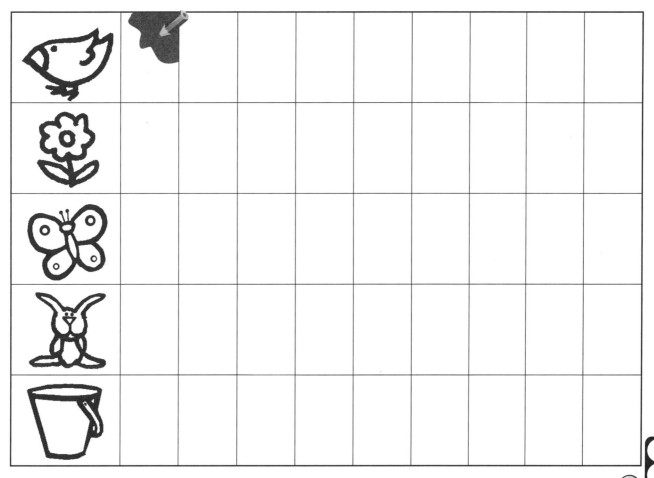

8 ## Let's Look Back

A **Fill in the missing numbers on the number strip.**

1	2		4		6		8		10

B

1	2	3	4	5	6	7	8	9	10

1. 2 + 5 = ☐

2. 2 + 3 = ☐

3. 4 + 4 = ☐

4. 3 + 5 = ☐

5. 5 + 4 = ☐

6. 3 + 4 = ☐

7. 1 + 7 = ☐

8. 5 + 2 = ☐

9. 6 + 3 = ☐

10. 2 + 7 = ☐

4 + 3 = 7

4 + 2 = ☐

2 + 1 = ☐

3 + 3 = ☐

C **Join up.**

2 + 3   4 + 4   2 + 2   5 + 1   4 + 5   3 + 4

8 6 5 7 4 9

D **Match the bags to the trolleys. Colour the same.**

4   3 + 1   2 + 3   5   6   3 + 4   5 + 3   7   8   4 + 2

Revision

A

| 1 | 2 | 3 | 4 | 5 | 6 | 7 | 8 | 9 | 10 |

1. 3
   + 4

2. 2
   + 7

3. 6
   + 2

4. 4
   + 2

5. 3
   + 5

6. 5
   + 4

7. 6
   + 3

8. 7
   + 3

9. 4
   + 5

10. 5
   + 5

11. 5
   + 3

12. 6
   + 1

B Match.

3
+ 2

4
+ 4

6
+ 3

9

5

8

C Add and colour.

7	
8	
9	
10	

5
+ 4

4
+ 3

8
+ 2

6
+ 2

6
+ 3

2
+ 7

7
+ 3

4
+ 5

Revision

Addition

When two numbers are added together, it doesn't matter which number comes first.

A **Warm-up. Listen to your teacher.**

1. ☐ 2. ☐ 3. ☐ 4. ☐ 5. ☐

=

2 + 3 = 5

3 + 2 = 5

B **Fill in the missing numbers.**

1. 6 + 3 = 3 + ☐	2. 4 + 2 = 2 + ☐
3. 5 + 2 = 2 + ☐	4. 7 + 3 = 3 + ☐

C **Draw the missing shapes.**

 + = + ☐

 + =  + ☐

 +  =  +  ☐

Objectives: Explore, develop and apply the commutative properties of addition.

Strand Number
Strand Unit Operations

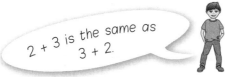

2 + 3 is the same as 3 + 2.

A Draw the missing fruits.

1. 🍎🍎🍎🍎🍎 + 🍎🍎🍎 = [ ] + 🍎🍎🍎🍎🍎

2. 🍐🍐🍐 + 🍐🍐🍐🍐🍐 = [ ] + 🍐🍐🍐

3. (6 bananas) + (2 bananas) = [ ] + (6 bananas)

4. 🍊🍊🍊 + 🍊🍊🍊🍊🍊🍊🍊 = [ ] + 🍊🍊🍊

B Fill in the missing numbers.

1. 2 + 4 = 4 + [ ]	2. [ ] + 5 = 5 + 8
3. 6 + 3 = 3 + [ ]	4. [ ] + 4 = 4 + 3
5. 5 + 2 = 2 + [ ]	6. [ ] + 1 = 1 + 9
7. 4 + 5 = 5 + [ ]	8. [ ] + 2 = 2 + 6
9. 3 + 7 = 7 + [ ]	10. [ ] + 3 = 3 + 6
11. 8 + 2 = 2 + [ ]	12. [ ] + 4 = 4 + 5

Objectives: Explore, develop and apply the commutative properties of addition.

Strand Number
Strand Unit Operations

The number stays the same when you add zero to it.

A **Fill in the missing numbers.**

1.   + | O | = | 2 |

2. | O | + = | |

3.  + | | = | 5 |

4. | O | +  = | |

B **Add.**

1.	4	2.	5	3.	O	4.	O	5.	7	6.	O
	+ O		+ O		+ 3		+ 8		+ O		+ 6

C **Fill in the missing numbers.**

1. 2 + O = | |

2. 9 + | | = 9

3. O + 10 = | |

4. O + | | = 4

5. O + 8 = | |

6. O + | | = 7

7. O + 3 = | |

8. 6 + | | = 6

9. 7 + O = | |

10. O + | | = 5

Objectives Explore, develop and apply the zero properties of addition.

Strand Number
Strand Unit Operations

I will learn about first to tenth.

A Warm-up. Listen to your teacher. **Use your counters.**

1st	2nd	3rd	4th	5th	6th	7th	8th	9th	10th
first	second	third	fourth	fifth	sixth	seventh	eighth	ninth	tenth

B Colour the second carriage green, the fifth red and the seventh blue.

C The first dancer is green. **Colour:**
- the sixth red.
- the eight blue.
- the tenth yellow.

D Circle the second last boy.

Tom   Pat   Liam   Sam

E Puzzle:
How many cubes?

There are ☐ cubes.

Objectives   Use the language of the ordinal number, first to tenth.

Strand	Number
Strand Unit	Comparing and Ordering

I will learn about the number 11.

A Write the number.

1 1 ☆ ☆ ☆ ☆ ☆

B Draw 11 🍎 on the tree.

C Join the dots. Colour.

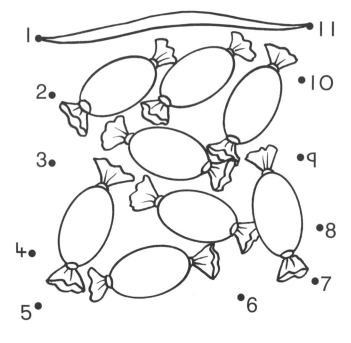

1 • 11
2 • • 10
3 • • 9
4 • • 8
• 7
5 • • 6

D Can you put the 11 cubes into the hoops in different ways?

+

Record your answers.

☐ + ☐ = 11	☐ + ☐ = 11	☐ + ☐ = 11
☐ + ☐ = 11	☐ + ☐ = 11	☐ + ☐ = 11
☐ + ☐ = 11	☐ + ☐ = 11	☐ + ☐ = 11

Objectives
• Explore, the additions combinations to make up the number 11.
• Develop an understanding of addition by combining or positioning sets. Use concrete materials.

| Strand | Number |
| Strand Unit | Operations |

I will learn about numbers that add to make 11.

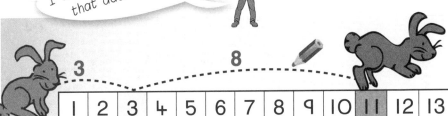

3   8

| 1 | 2 | 3 | 4 | 5 | 6 | 7 | 8 | 9 | 10 | 11 | 12 | 13 | 14 | 15 | 16 | 17 | 18 | 19 | 20 |

$3 + 8 = 11$

A Use the number strip to do these.

1. $8 + 3 = \boxed{}$ 2. $4 + \boxed{} = 11$ 3. $\boxed{} + 6 = 11$

4. $2 + 9 = \boxed{}$ 5. $7 + \boxed{} = 11$ 6. $\boxed{} + 1 = 11$

7. $6 + 5 = \boxed{}$ 8. $10 + \boxed{} = 11$ 9. $\boxed{} + 3 = 11$

B Use the number strip or counters to do these.

1. 8   2. 6   3. 9   4. 10   5. 4   6. 7
   + 3   + 5   + 2   + $\boxed{}$ + $\boxed{}$ + $\boxed{}$
   $\boxed{}$ $\boxed{}$ $\boxed{}$ 11   11   11

C Use 11 cubes to find ways to make 11.

Pair work

$\bigcirc + \bigcirc + \bigcirc$

1. Record your answers.

$\boxed{} + \boxed{} + \boxed{} = 11$

$\boxed{} + \boxed{} + \boxed{} = 11$

$\boxed{} + \boxed{} + \boxed{} = 11$

$\boxed{} + \boxed{} + \boxed{} = 11$

2. Try these.

$1 + 2 + \boxed{} = 11$

$3 + 1 + \boxed{} = 11$

$4 + 5 + \boxed{} = 11$

$3 + 7 + \boxed{} = 11$

Objectives
• Add numbers without renaming within 20.
• Develop an understanding of addition by combining or partitioning sets, use concrete materials.

Strand   Number
Strand Unit   Operations

Twelve 12

I will learn about the number 12.

A **Write the number.**

12 12 12 12 12 12 12

B Draw 12 🐟.

C Join the dots from 1 to 12. Colour the picture.

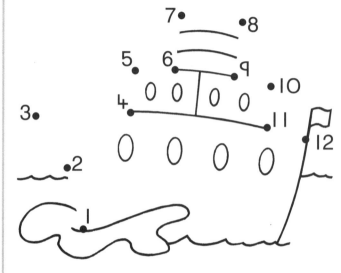

D Can you put 12 cubes into the hoops in different ways?

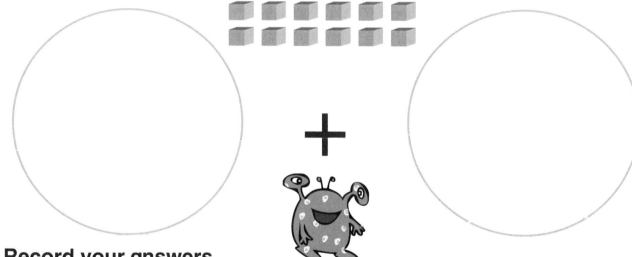

+

Record your answers.

☐ + ☐ = 12	☐ + ☐ = 12	☐ + ☐ = 12
☐ + ☐ = 12	☐ + ☐ = 12	☐ + ☐ = 12
☐ + ☐ = 12	☐ + ☐ = 12	☐ + ☐ = 12

I will learn about numbers that add to make 12.

5   7

| 1 | 2 | 3 | 4 | 5 | 6 | 7 | 8 | 9 | 10 | 11 | 12 | 13 | 14 | 15 | 16 | 17 | 18 | 19 | 20 |

$$5 + 7 = 12$$

A Use the number strip to do these.

1. $10 + 2 = \boxed{}$ 2. $8 + \boxed{} = 12$ 3. $\boxed{} + 7 = 12$

4. $5 + 7 = \boxed{}$ 5. $3 + \boxed{} = 12$ 6. $\boxed{} + 8 = 12$

7. $9 + 3 = \boxed{}$ 8. $12 + \boxed{} = 12$ 9. $\boxed{} + 6 = 12$

B Use the number strip or counters to do these.

1. $\begin{array}{r} 8 \\ + 4 \\ \hline \boxed{} \end{array}$
2. $\begin{array}{r} 7 \\ + 5 \\ \hline \boxed{} \end{array}$
3. $\begin{array}{r} 3 \\ + 9 \\ \hline \boxed{} \end{array}$
4. $\begin{array}{r} 2 \\ + \boxed{} \\ \hline 12 \end{array}$
5. $\begin{array}{r} 10 \\ + \boxed{} \\ \hline 12 \end{array}$
6. $\begin{array}{r} 7 \\ + \boxed{} \\ \hline 12 \end{array}$

C Use 12 cubes to make 12.

Pair work

$\bigcirc \quad + \quad \bigcirc \quad + \quad \bigcirc$

1. **Record your answers.**

$\boxed{} + \boxed{} + \boxed{} = 12$

$\boxed{} + \boxed{} + \boxed{} = 12$

$\boxed{} + \boxed{} + \boxed{} = 12$

$\boxed{} + \boxed{} + \boxed{} = 12$

2. **Try these.**

$4 + 0 + \boxed{} = 12$

$6 + 3 + \boxed{} = 12$

$1 + 7 + \boxed{} = 12$

$3 + 4 + \boxed{} = 12$

I will learn about the number 13.

A Write the number.

13

B Colour only 13 birds.

C Can you put 13 cubes into the hoops in different ways?

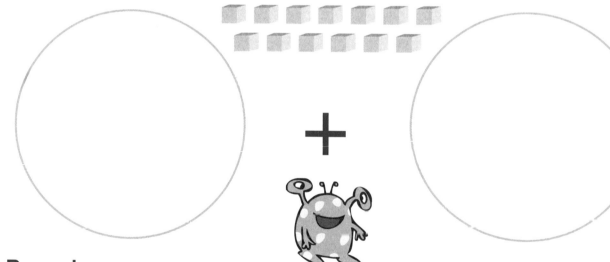

+

Record your answers.

☐ + ☐ = 13   ☐ + ☐ = 13   ☐ + ☐ = 13

☐ + ☐ = 13   ☐ + ☐ = 13   ☐ + ☐ = 13

☐ + ☐ = 13   ☐ + ☐ = 13   ☐ + ☐ = 13

Objectives — Develop an understanding of addition by combining or partitioning sets, use concrete materials.

Strand   Number
Strand Unit   Operations

I will learn about numbers that add to make 13.

8   5

| 1 | 2 | 3 | 4 | 5 | 6 | 7 | 8 | 9 | 10 | 11 | 12 | 13 | 14 | 15 | 16 | 17 | 18 | 19 | 20 |

8 + 5 = 13

A Use the number strip to do these.

1. 11 + 2 = ☐   2. 5 + ☐ = 13   3. ☐ + 3 = 13

4. 9 + 4 = ☐   5. 1 + ☐ = 13   6. ☐ + 9 = 13

7. 6 + 7 = ☐   8. 7 + ☐ = 13   9. ☐ + 6 = 13

B Use the number strip or counters to do these.

1.   10   2.   2   3.   8   4.   6   5.   12   6.   1

   + 3   + 11   + 5   + ☐   + ☐   + ☐
   ─────   ─────   ─────   ─────   ─────   ─────
   ☐   ☐   ☐   13   13   13

C Use 13 cubes to make 13.

Pair work

 +  + ◯

1.   **Record your answers.**

☐ + ☐ + ☐ = 13

☐ + ☐ + ☐ = 13

☐ + ☐ + ☐ = 13

☐ + ☐ + ☐ = 13

2.   **Try these.**

6 + ☐ + 5 = 13

3 + ☐ + 7 = 13

7 + ☐ + 4 = 13

8 + ☐ + 2 = 13

Objectives
• Add numbers without renaming within 20.
• Develop an understanding of addition by combining or partitioning sets, use concrete materials.

Strand	Number
Strand Unit	Addition

I will learn about the number 14.

A **Write the number.**

14 14 14 14 14 14

B Draw 14 ⭐ in the sky. One has been drawn for you.

C Can you put 14 cubes into the hoops in different ways?

Record your answers.

☐ + ☐ = 14   ☐ + ☐ = 14   ☐ + ☐ = 14

☐ + ☐ = 14   ☐ + ☐ = 14   ☐ + ☐ = 14

☐ + ☐ = 14   ☐ + ☐ = 14   ☐ + ☐ = 14

Objectives: Develop an understanding of addition by combining or partitioning sets, use concrete materials.

Strand Number
Strand Unit Operations

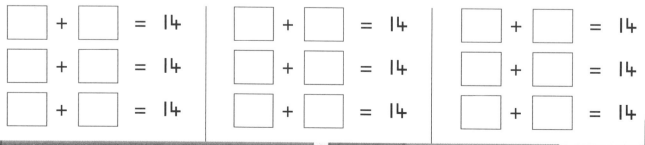

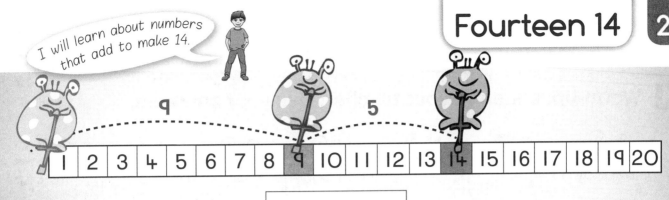

I will learn about numbers that add to make 14.

$9 + 5 = 14$

A Use the number strip to do these.

1. $10 + 4 = \boxed{}$
2. $7 + \boxed{} = 14$
3. $\boxed{} + 12 = 14$

4. $5 + 9 = \boxed{}$
5. $6 + \boxed{} = 14$
6. $\boxed{} + 14 = 14$

7. $3 + 11 = \boxed{}$
8. $4 + \boxed{} = 14$
9. $\boxed{} + 7 = 14$

B Use the number strip or counters to do these.

1. $\begin{array}{r} 7 \\ + 7 \\ \hline \boxed{} \end{array}$
2. $\begin{array}{r} 8 \\ + 6 \\ \hline \boxed{} \end{array}$
3. $\begin{array}{r} 4 \\ + 10 \\ \hline \boxed{} \end{array}$
4. $\begin{array}{r} 14 \\ + \boxed{} \\ \hline 14 \end{array}$
5. $\begin{array}{r} 2 \\ + \boxed{} \\ \hline 14 \end{array}$
6. $\begin{array}{r} 9 \\ + \boxed{} \\ \hline 14 \end{array}$

C Use 14 cubes to make 14.

Pair work

$\bigcirc + \bigcirc + \bigcirc$

1. Record your answers.

$\boxed{} + \boxed{} + \boxed{} = 14$

$\boxed{} + \boxed{} + \boxed{} = 14$

$\boxed{} + \boxed{} + \boxed{} = 14$

$\boxed{} + \boxed{} + \boxed{} = 14$

2. Try these.

$3 + \boxed{} + 3 = 14$

$2 + \boxed{} + 5 = 14$

$7 + \boxed{} + 3 = 14$

$8 + \boxed{} + 2 = 14$

Time

I will learn the days of the week.

A **Warm-up. Listen to your teacher. Use your counters.**

Monday | Tuesday | Wednesday | Thursday | Friday | Saturday | Sunday

B 1. _____ comes before Wednesday.

2. _____ comes after Thursday.

3. _____ is my favourite day.

4. Tomorrow will be _____.

5. Yesterday was _____.

C

| Mon | Tues | Wed | Thurs | Fri | Sat | Sun |

Write the days.

Football is on _____   Library is on _____

Music is on _____   Drama is on _____

The hike is on _____   PE is on _____

Art is on _____

| Strand | Measures |
| Strand Unit | Time |

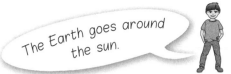

The Earth goes around the sun.

A Write the correct word.

| m_____ | a_____ | e_____ | n_____ |

morning
afternoon
evening
night

Fill in the missing words.

1. I sleep during the _____.
2. I arrive at school in the _____.
3. I leave school in the _____.
4. The sun goes down in the _____.

B Write 1, 2, 3 or 4 in the boxes.

A. [ ] [ ] [ ] [2]

B. [ ] [ ] [ ] [ ]

C. [ ] [ ] [ ] [ ]

C Draw what happens next.

Objectives: Use the vocabulary of time to sequence events.

| Strand | Measures |
| Strand Unit | Time |

I will learn about the number 15.

A **Write the number.**

15 15 15 15 15 15 15

B **Write the missing numbers on the train.**

1   5   10   15

C **How many bees can you see?** ☐

D **Can you put 15 cubes into the hoops in different ways?**

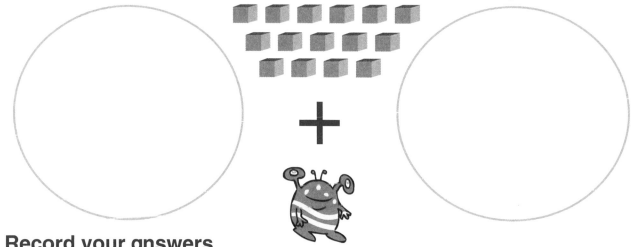

+

Record your answers.

☐ + ☐ = 15   ☐ + ☐ = 15   ☐ + ☐ = 15

☐ + ☐ = 15   ☐ + ☐ = 15   ☐ + ☐ = 15

☐ + ☐ = 15   ☐ + ☐ = 15   ☐ + ☐ = 15

Objectives Develop an understanding of addition by combining or partitioning sets, use concrete materials.

Strand Number
Strand Unit Operations

I will learn about numbers that add to make 15.

| 1 | 2 | 3 | 4 | 5 | 6 | 7 | 8 | 9 | 10 | 11 | 12 | 13 | 14 | 15 | 16 | 17 | 18 | 19 | 20 |

4   11

$$4 + 11 = 15$$

A Use the number strip to do these.

1. $6 + 9 = \boxed{}$ 2. $10 + \boxed{} = 15$ 3. $\boxed{} + 1 = 15$

4. $8 + 7 = \boxed{}$ 5. $3 + \boxed{} = 15$ 6. $\boxed{} + 4 = 15$

7. $11 + 4 = \boxed{}$ 8. $13 + \boxed{} = 15$ 9. $\boxed{} + 8 = 15$

B Use the number strip or counters to do these.

1.	2.	3.	4.	5.	6.
5	7	6	8	4	1
+ 10	+ 8	+ 9	+ ☐	+ ☐	+ ☐
☐	☐	☐	15	15	15

C Use 15 cubes to make 15.

Pair work

◯ ➕ ◯ ➕ ◯

1. Record your answers.

$\boxed{} + \boxed{} + \boxed{} = 15$

$\boxed{} + \boxed{} + \boxed{} = 15$

$\boxed{} + \boxed{} + \boxed{} = 15$

$\boxed{} + \boxed{} + \boxed{} = 15$

2. Try these.

$7 + \boxed{} + 7 = 15$

$4 + \boxed{} + 3 = 15$

$5 + \boxed{} + 5 = 15$

$9 + \boxed{} + 6 = 15$

Objectives
• Add numbers without renaming within 20.
• Develop an understanding of addition by combining or partitioning sets, use concrete materials.

Strand	Number
Strand Unit	Addition

I will learn about the number 16.

A Write the number.

16 16 16 16 16 16

B Count the shapes. How many?

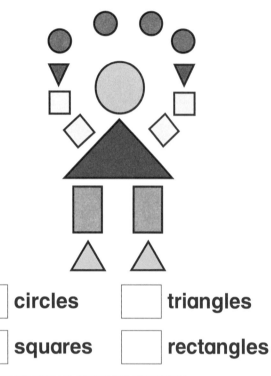

☐ circles ☐ triangles

☐ squares ☐ rectangles

C Join the dots from 1 to 16. Colour the picture.

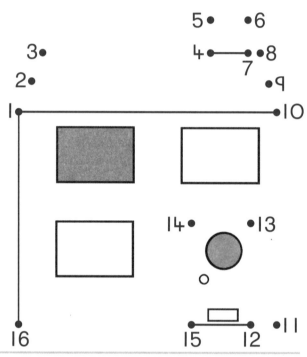

D Can you put 16 cubes into the hoops in different ways?

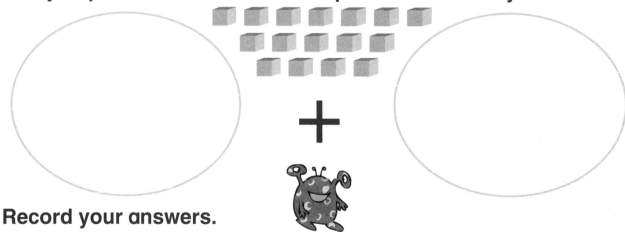

+

Record your answers.

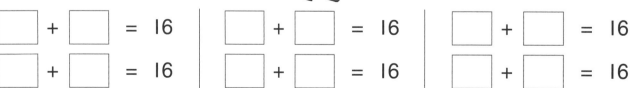

☐ + ☐ = 16	☐ + ☐ = 16	☐ + ☐ = 16
☐ + ☐ = 16	☐ + ☐ = 16	☐ + ☐ = 16
☐ + ☐ = 16	☐ + ☐ = 16	☐ + ☐ = 16

Objectives — Develop an understanding of addition by combining or partitioning sets, use concrete materials.

Strand Number
Strand Unit Operations

I will learn about numbers that add to make 16.

| 1 | 2 | 3 | 4 | 5 | 6 | 7 | 8 | 9 | 10 | 11 | 12 | 13 | 14 | 15 | 16 | 17 | 18 | 19 | 20 |

$$8 + 8 = 16$$

A Use the number strip to do these.

1. $12 + 4 = \boxed{}$ 2. $10 + \boxed{} = 16$ 3. $\boxed{} + 14 = 16$

4. $11 + 5 = \boxed{}$ 5. $1 + \boxed{} = 16$ 6. $\boxed{} + 12 = 16$

7. $9 + 7 = \boxed{}$ 8. $4 + \boxed{} = 16$ 9. $\boxed{} + 7 = 16$

B Use the number strip or counters to do these.

1. $\begin{array}{r} 2 \\ + 14 \\ \hline \boxed{} \end{array}$ 2. $\begin{array}{r} 0 \\ + 16 \\ \hline \boxed{} \end{array}$ 3. $\begin{array}{r} 8 \\ + 8 \\ \hline \boxed{} \end{array}$ 4. $\begin{array}{r} 9 \\ + \boxed{} \\ \hline 16 \end{array}$ 5. $\begin{array}{r} 15 \\ + \boxed{} \\ \hline 16 \end{array}$ 6. $\begin{array}{r} 6 \\ + \boxed{} \\ \hline 16 \end{array}$

C Pair work 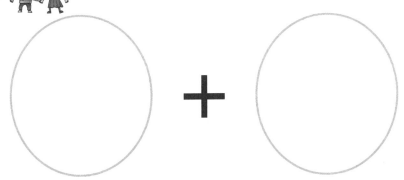 Use 16 cubes to make 16.

$$\bigcirc \quad + \quad \bigcirc \quad + \quad \bigcirc$$

1. Record your answers.

$\boxed{} + \boxed{} + \boxed{} = 16$

$\boxed{} + \boxed{} + \boxed{} = 16$

$\boxed{} + \boxed{} + \boxed{} = 16$

$\boxed{} + \boxed{} + \boxed{} = 16$

2. Try these.

$9 + \boxed{} + 1 = 16$

$6 + \boxed{} + 3 = 16$

$7 + \boxed{} + 5 = 16$

$8 + \boxed{} + 8 = 16$

Objectives
• Add numbers without renaming within 20.
• Develop an understanding of addition by combining or partitioning sets, use concrete materials.

Strand   Number
Strand Unit   Operations

A 1. Colour only 5 apples **red**.

2. Fill in the missing numbers.

3. Write 2 ways to make 8.

⬜ + ⬜ = 8

⬜ + ⬜ = 8

4. 5 + 2 = 2 + ⬜

5. How many days in a week? ⬜

6. Colour the 2nd person **green**.

7. Colour the 4th person **blue**.

8. 10 + ⬜ = 16

[8]

B 1. 2 + ⬜ + 3 = 10

2. Order the pictures 1 to 3 starting with what you might eat first during the day.

3. Colour only 6 sweets **yellow**.

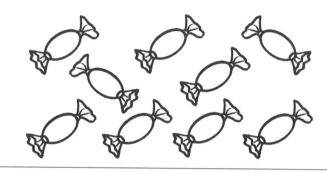

4. Write the correct answer.

I wake up in the ⬜.

morning   afternoon   night

5. 8 + 0 = ⬜

6. Match.

eight   9
four   3
nine   8
three   4

7. 3 + 6 = 6 + ⬜

8. Draw the hands to show 3 o'clock.

[8]

Making 10

There are pairs of numbers that make ten, which can make it easier for us when we are adding.

$1 + 9 = 10$ $9 + 1 = 10$

$2 + 8 = 10$ $8 + 2 = 10$

$3 + 7 = 10$ $7 + 3 = 10$

$4 + 6 = 10$ $6 + 4 = 10$

$5 + 5 = 10$ $10 + 0 = 10$

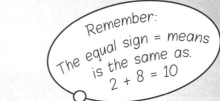

Remember:
The equal sign = means is the same as.
$2 + 8 = 10$

Find the pairs that make 10, then add the other number.

Example:

A | 2 | + | 8 | + | 3 | = | 10 | + | 3 | = | 13 |

B | 3 | + | 4 | + | 7 | = | 10 | + | 4 | = | 14 |

A

1. | 6 | + | 4 | + | 5 | = | 10 | + | 5 | = | 15 |

2. | 8 | + | 3 | + | 2 | = | 10 | + | | = | 13 |

3. | 5 | + | 4 | + | 6 | = | | + | 5 | = | 15 |

4. | 5 | + | 9 | + | 1 | = | | + | 5 | = | 15 |

5. | 8 | + | 6 | + | 2 | = | | + | | = | 16 |

6. | 1 | + | 7 | + | 9 | = | | + | 7 | = | |

7. | 4 | + | 8 | + | 2 | = | | + | 4 | = | |

8. | 7 | + | 8 | + | 3 | = | | + | | = | |

9. | 8 | + | 9 | + | 1 | = | | + | | = | |

10. | 6 | + | 5 | + | 4 | = | | + | | = | |

The Farmyard

Find the . Circle it green.

Find the . Circle him blue.

1. How many ? ☐

2. How many ? ☐

3. How many ? ☐

4. How many ? ☐

5. How many and ?

☐ + ☐ = ☐

6. How many and ?

☐ + ☐ = ☐

7. Find the shapes in the picture.
Tick them when you find them.

■ ☐

▢ ☐

△ ☐

8. How many ? ☐

9. How many and ?

☐ + ☐ = ☐

10. How many ? ☐

11. Are there more then ?

☐ yes ☐ no

Find the . Circle it red.

Problem Solving 1

1 Ann had **6** dinosaurs and she was given **4** more. How many does she have **altogether**? ☐ + ☐ = ☐

2 Granny gave Tom **15 cent** and on the way home he lost **5 cent**. How much does he have now? ☐ c

3 Jean bought a comic for **10 cent** and a packet of crisps for **10 cent**. How much did she spend? ☐ c

4 A bus ride costs **10 cent**. How much will it cost for two children? ☐ c

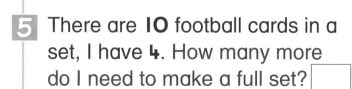

5 There are **10** football cards in a set, I have **4**. How many more do I need to make a full set? ☐

6 Helen has **4** dolls. Anita has **10** dolls. How many more dolls has Anita? ☐

7 Michael has **9** cars in his collection. Ann has **12** in her collection. How many fewer cars has Michael? ☐

8 **Puzzle:** Find 8 differences. X them. Colour the second picture.

I will learn about 2D shapes.

A Warm-up. Listen to your teacher. Use your counters.

B Name the shapes. Colour.

_____ _____ _____ _____ _____

rectangle, square, triangle, circle, semi-circle

C How many?

1. A triangle has ☐ sides.

2. A square has ☐ corners.

3. A rectangle has ☐ sides.

4. A circle has ☐ corners.

D Colour.

1. Colour the ■.

2. Colour the ▬.

3. Colour the ●.

4. Colour the △.

E Draw.

1. Draw a circle inside the triangle.

2. Draw a rectangle beside the triangle.

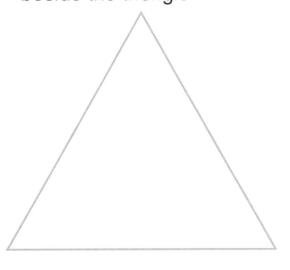

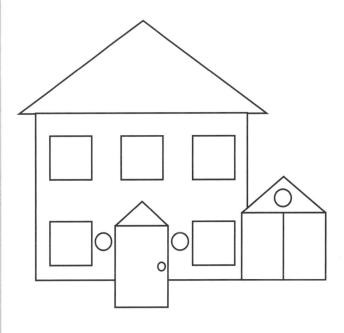

Objectives
• Sort, describe, compare and name 2D shapes: square, rectangle, triangle, circle, semi-circle.
• Construct and draw 2D shapes.

Strand	Shape and Space
Strand Unit	2D Shapes

34 **2D Shapes**

I can draw pictures using 2D shapes.

A

1. Colour the ■.

2. Colour the ▬.

3. Colour the ●.

4. Colour the △.

B How many?

1. There are ☐ squares in the boat.

2. There are ☐ circles in the boat.

3. There are ☐ rectangles in the robot.

4. There are ☐ triangles in the two pictures.

5. There are ☐ more circles than semi-circles in the robot.

6. Pick your own colours. Colour the pictures.

C Draw your own shape picture, using ▬, ○ and △. Colour.

Objectives
• Identify and discuss the use of 2D shapes in the environment.
• Combine and partition 2D shapes.
• Construct and draw 2D shapes.

Strand Shape and Space
Strand Unit 2D Shapes

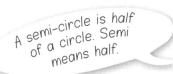
A semi-circle is half of a circle. Semi means half.

A True or false? ✓ or ✗. Colour.

Count

1. There are **10** circles.

2. There are more than **8** triangles.

3. There are **5** more rectangles than circles.

4. There are **2** less squares than circles.

5. There are **14** triangles and circles altogether.

B Make a block graph of the picture above. Colour.

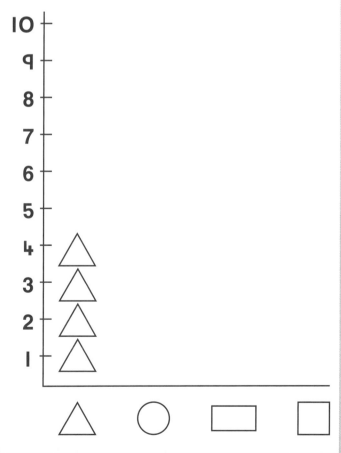

10
9
8
7
6
5
4
3
2
1

C Puzzle: Colour half of each shape.

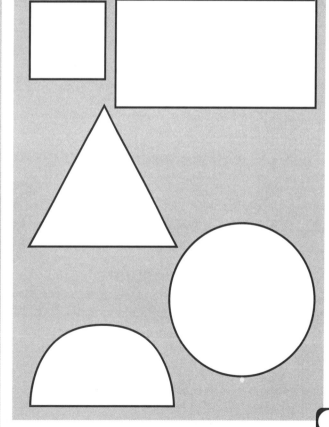

Objectives
• Sort, describe, compare and name 2D shapes: square, rectangle, triangle, circle, semi-circle.
• Identify halves of 2D shapes.

Strand Shape and Space
Strand Unit 2D Shapes

Seventeen 17

I will learn about the number 17.

A Draw 17 .

B Write the number.

17 17 17 17 17 17 17

C Can you put 17 cubes into the hoops in different ways?

+

Record your answers.

□ + □ = 17	□ + □ = 17	□ + □ = 17
□ + □ = 17	□ + □ = 17	□ + □ = 17
□ + □ = 17	□ + □ = 17	□ + □ = 17

Objectives Develop an understanding of addition by combining or partitioning sets, use concrete materials.

| **Strand** | Number |
| **Strand Unit** | Operations |

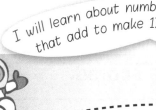 I will learn about numbers that add to make 17.

10

7

| 1 | 2 | 3 | 4 | 5 | 6 | 7 | 8 | 9 | 10 | 11 | 12 | 13 | 14 | 15 | 16 | 17 | 18 | 19 | 20 |

$$10 + 7 = 17$$

A   Use the number strip to do these.

1. $5 + 12 = \boxed{}$ 2. $4 + \boxed{} = 17$ 3. $\boxed{} + 7 = 17$

4. $16 + 1 = \boxed{}$ 5. $2 + \boxed{} = 17$ 6. $\boxed{} + 11 = 17$

7. $7 + 10 = \boxed{}$ 8. $8 + \boxed{} = 17$ 9. $\boxed{} + 8 = 17$

B   Use the number strip or counters to do these.

1. $\begin{array}{r} 13 \\ + 4 \\ \hline \boxed{} \end{array}$ 2. $\begin{array}{r} 0 \\ + 17 \\ \hline \boxed{} \end{array}$ 3. $\begin{array}{r} 9 \\ + 8 \\ \hline \boxed{} \end{array}$ 4. $\begin{array}{r} 7 \\ + \boxed{} \\ \hline 17 \end{array}$ 5. $\begin{array}{r} 5 \\ + \boxed{} \\ \hline 17 \end{array}$ 6. $\begin{array}{r} 11 \\ + \boxed{} \\ \hline 17 \end{array}$

C   Use 17 cubes to make 17.

 Pair work

$\bigcirc + \bigcirc + \bigcirc$

1. **Record your answers.**

$\boxed{} + \boxed{} + \boxed{} = 17$

$\boxed{} + \boxed{} + \boxed{} = 17$

$\boxed{} + \boxed{} + \boxed{} = 17$

$\boxed{} + \boxed{} + \boxed{} = 17$

2. **Try these.**

$6 + \boxed{} + 5 = 17$

$7 + \boxed{} + 2 = 17$

$4 + \boxed{} + 9 = 17$

$1 + \boxed{} + 5 = 17$

Objectives
• Add numbers without renaming within 20.
• Develop an understanding of addition by combining or partitioning sets, use concrete materials.

Strand	Number
Strand Unit	Operations

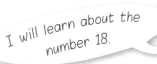
I will learn about the number 18.

A Draw 18 balls ⚽ in the picture. Only 5 goals are scored.

B Write the number.

C Can you put 18 cubes into the hoops in different ways?

 **+**

Record your answers.

☐ + ☐ = 18		☐ + ☐ = 18		☐ + ☐ = 18
☐ + ☐ = 18		☐ + ☐ = 18		☐ + ☐ = 18
☐ + ☐ = 18		☐ + ☐ = 18		☐ + ☐ = 18

Objectives Develop an understanding of addition by combining or partitioning sets, use concrete materials.

Strand Number
Strand Unit Operations

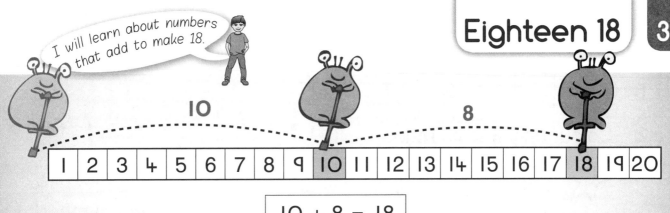

$$10 + 8 = 18$$

A Use the number strip to do these.

1. $7 + 11 = \boxed{}$ 2. $1 + \boxed{} = 18$ 3. $\boxed{} + 14 = 18$

4. $2 + 16 = \boxed{}$ 5. $0 + \boxed{} = 18$ 6. $\boxed{} + 10 = 18$

7. $9 + 9 = \boxed{}$ 8. $5 + \boxed{} = 18$ 9. $\boxed{} + 2 = 18$

B Use the number strip or counters to do these.

1. $3 + 15 = \boxed{}$ 2. $16 + 2 = \boxed{}$ 3. $12 + 6 = \boxed{}$ 4. $9 + \boxed{} = 18$ 5. $14 + \boxed{} = 18$ 6. $18 + \boxed{} = 18$

C Use 18 cubes to make 18.

Pair work

◯ + ◯ + ◯

1. Record your answers.

$\boxed{} + \boxed{} + \boxed{} = 18$

$\boxed{} + \boxed{} + \boxed{} = 18$

$\boxed{} + \boxed{} + \boxed{} = 18$

$\boxed{} + \boxed{} + \boxed{} = 18$

2. Try these.

$4 + \boxed{} + 5 = 18$

$10 + \boxed{} + 3 = 18$

$5 + \boxed{} + 5 = 18$

$2 + \boxed{} + 9 = 18$

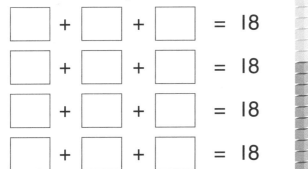

- Add numbers without renaming within 20.
- Develop an understanding of addition by combining or partitioning sets, use concrete materials.

| Strand | Number |
| Strand Unit | Operations |

A

1. $5 + \boxed{} = 2 + 7$

2. Colour only 8 stars **blue**.

3. How many circles are in this picture?

$\boxed{}$

4. Write 2 ways to make 16.

$\boxed{} + \boxed{} = 16$

$\boxed{} + \boxed{} = 16$

5. $4 + \boxed{} = 10$

6. How many corners has a rectangle? $\boxed{}$

7. $7 + 2 = \boxed{} + 7$

8. What time is it?

_____ | $\boxed{8}$

B

1.

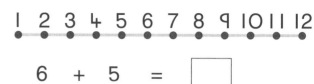

$6 + 5 = \boxed{}$

2. Circle the biggest number.

4   7   5   8   10   6

3. 2nd comes after _____.

4. Put an X on the shape that has no corners.

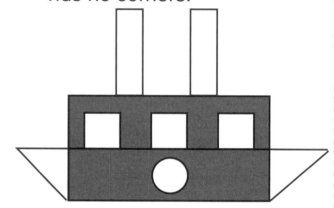

5. **True or false? ✓ or x.**

A semi-circle has 2 corners. $\boxed{}$

A circle has 4 corners. $\boxed{}$

A triangle has 6 sides. $\boxed{}$

A square has 4 sides. $\boxed{}$

6. $10 + 0 = \boxed{}$

7. $\boxed{} + 9 = 17$

8. Show 7 o'clock.

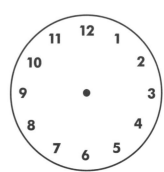

$\boxed{8}$

Doubles

When we add two numbers that are the same we call them doubles.

1	+	1	=	2
2	+	2	=	4
3	+	3	=	6
4	+	4	=	8
5	+	5	=	10

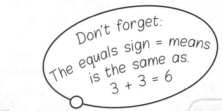

Don't forget:
The equals sign = means
is the same as.
3 + 3 = 6

6	+	6	=	12
7	+	7	=	14
8	+	8	=	16
9	+	9	=	18
10	+	10	=	20

A Look at these sums and decide if they are doubles. Circle the doubles. Do all the sums.

1. 4 + 4 = ☐   2 + 2 = ☐   5 + 2 = ☐

    7 + 1 = ☐   5 + 5 = ☐   1 + 1 = ☐

2. 8 + 8 = ☐   8 + 2 = ☐   6 + 6 = ☐

    4 + 8 = ☐   9 + 9 = ☐   6 + 3 = ☐

3. 3 + 8 = ☐   7 + 7 = ☐   3 + 2 = ☐

    6 + 6 = ☐   4 + 7 = ☐   3 + 3 = ☐

B See how quickly you can answer these.

1. 2 + 2 = ☐   3 + 3 = ☐   4 + 4 = ☐

2. 8 + 8 = ☐   5 + 5 = ☐   9 + 9 = ☐

3. 9 + 9 = ☐   6 + 6 = ☐   3 + 3 = ☐

4. 1 + 1 = ☐   7 + 7 = ☐   10 + 10 = ☐

Problem Solving 2

1 **Find the hidden numbers from 1 to 20. X them. Colour.**

Maths is fun!

C **Puzzle: Finish the walls.**

3 **Join the dots. Colour.**

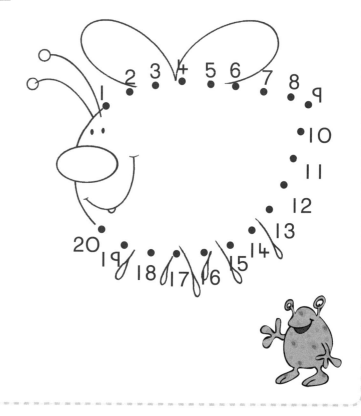

43 | # More Than

9 is more than 4.

A More than.

1.

 has ☐ more than.

2.

 has ☐ more than.

3.

 has ☐ more than.

4.

 has ☐ more than.

B Try these.

1. There are ☐ more cats than dogs.

2. There are ☐ more cars than bikes.

C Puzzle: Write the number that is 3 more.

1. (4) ——3——→ (7)

2. (6) ——→ ( )

3. (5) ——→ ( )

4. (3) ——→ ( )

5. (0) ——→ ( )

Objectives Compare equivalent and non-equivalent sets: name the inequality.

Strand Number
Strand Unit Comparing and Ordering

A Less than.

1.     has ☐ less than 👧.

2.     has ☐ less than 👧.

3.     has ☐ less than 👦.

4.     has ☐ less than 👧.

B Try these.

1. There are ☐ less 🐛 than 🦋.

2. There is ☐ less 🦁 than 🐪.

C Puzzle: Write the number that is 2 less.

1.  (5) ← (7)

2.  ( ) ← (4)

3.  ( ) ← (9)

4.  ( ) ← (6)

5.  ( ) ← (8)

Objectives
• Compare equivalent and non-equivalent sets.
• Order sets of objects by number.

Strand Number
Strand Unit Comparing and Ordering

I will answer questions about pictures.

A Warm-up. Listen to your teacher. Use your counters.

 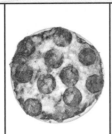    

B Lunch time

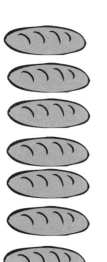      

| roll | sandwich | pie | sausage roll | salad |

1. How many children had a sandwich for lunch? _____
2. How many children had a pie? _____
3. How many children had a sausage roll? _____
4. Did more children have a pie than a salad? _____
5. Did fewer children have a roll than a pie? _____

C Circle the healthy foods green.
Circle the unhealthy foods red.

Objectives: Represent and interpret data in two, three or four rows or columns using real objects, models and pictures.

| Strand | Data |
| Strand Unit | Representing and Interpreting Data |

I will answer questions about pictures.

A Colour the correct number of blocks. One is done for you.

▓				
▓				
▓				
▓				
▓				
▓				
🐵	🦒	🐍	🦁	🐘

1. How many 🦒 ?
2. How many 🐵 ?
3. How many 🐘 ?
4. How many 🦁 and 🐍 ?

B Puzzle: Which animal is the odd one out? Circle it.

Objectives
• Represent and interpret data in two, three or four rows or columns using real objects, models and pictures.
• Sort and classify objects by two and three criteria.

Strand	Data
Strand Unit	Representing and Interpreting Data

A Tara carried out a traffic study. She wrote down the colours of the cars that passed her house. Colour the blocks to show the results.

car colour	blue	green	black	red
number of cars	6	8	9	4

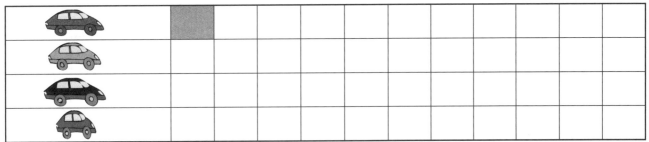

B 1. How many more green cars than red cars?

2. How many more black cars than red cars?

3. How many more blue cars than red cars?

4. How many more green cars than blue cars?

C Sean's class drew a picture of their favourite fruit.

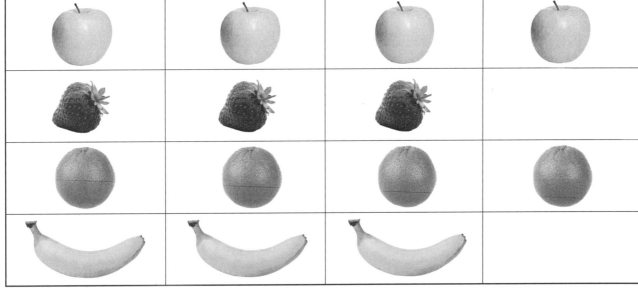

1. How many like apples and bananas?

2. How many like oranges and apples?

3. How many more like apples than bananas?

4. How many more like oranges than strawberries?

Objectives: Represent and interpret data in two, three or four rows or columns using real objects, models and pictures.

Strand   Data
Strand Unit   Representing and Interpreting Data

A Colour the picture.

Count, then colour the correct number of blocks.										How many?
🐑										
🐓										
🐴										
🐷										
🐴										

B True or false? ✓ or ✗.

1. There are more 🐑 than 🐴 . ▢
2. There are more 🐷 than 🐴 . ▢
3. There are less 🐴 than 🐓 . ▢
4. There are less 🐴 than 🐷 . ▢

Objectives
• Represent and interpret data in two, three or four rows or columns using real objects, models and pictures.
• Sort and classify objects by two and three criteria.

I will learn about a calendar.

A Fill in the missing numbers on the calendar.

June						
Monday	Tuesday	Wednesday	Thursday	Friday	Saturday	Sunday
				1		
4	5		7	8	9	
11	12		14	15	16	17
18	19		21	22	23	24
25	26		28	29	30	

1. How many days in June? ☐   2. How many sunny days? ☐

3. How many Fridays? ☐   4. How many cloudy days ☐

B Colour the blocks to show the weather in June.

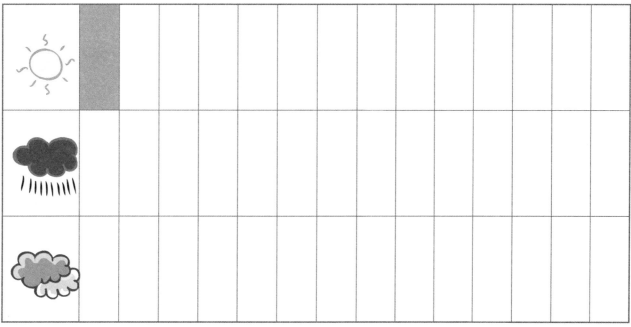

• Represent and interpret data in two, three or four rows or columns using real objects, models and pictures.
• Sort and classify objects by two and three criteria.

Strand   Measures
Strand Unit   Money

I will learn about the number 19.

A Write the missing numbers.

| 1 | 2 | 3 | | 5 | 6 | 7 | | 9 | 10 | | 12 | | 14 | | 16 | 17 | 18 | 19 | 20 |

B Write the number.

C

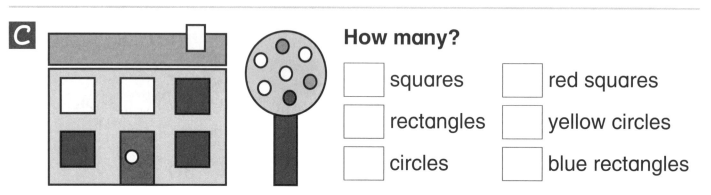

How many?

	squares		red squares
	rectangles		yellow circles
	circles		blue rectangles

D Can you put 19 cubes into the hoops in different ways?

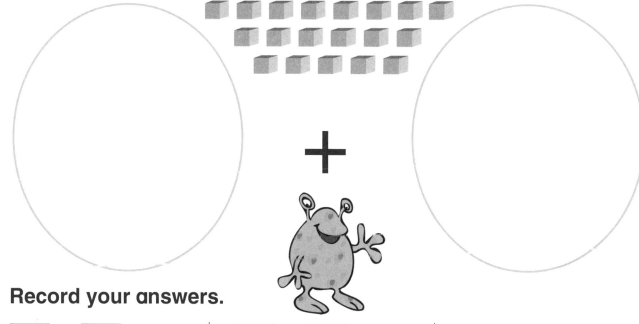

+

Record your answers.

☐ + ☐ = 19   ☐ + ☐ = 19   ☐ + ☐ = 19

☐ + ☐ = 19   ☐ + ☐ = 19   ☐ + ☐ = 19

☐ + ☐ = 19   ☐ + ☐ = 19   ☐ + ☐ = 19

Objectives — Develop an understanding of addition by combining or partitioning sets, use concrete materials.

Strand Number
Strand Unit Operations

I will learn about numbers that add to make 19.

10   9

| 1 | 2 | 3 | 4 | 5 | 6 | 7 | 8 | 9 | 10 | 11 | 12 | 13 | 14 | 15 | 16 | 17 | 18 | 19 | 20 |

$$10 + 9 = 19$$

A Use the number strip to do these.

1. $0 + 19 = \boxed{}$

2. $11 + \boxed{} = 19$

3. $\boxed{} + 5 = 19$

4. $4 + 15 = \boxed{}$

5. $2 + \boxed{} = 19$

6. $\boxed{} + 2 = 19$

7. $9 + 10 = \boxed{}$

8. $7 + \boxed{} = 19$

9. $\boxed{} + 9 = 19$

B Use the number strip or counters to do these.

1.
$$
\begin{array}{r}
14 \\
+\ 5 \\
\hline
\boxed{}
\end{array}
$$

2.
$$
\begin{array}{r}
16 \\
+\ 3 \\
\hline
\boxed{}
\end{array}
$$

3.
$$
\begin{array}{r}
10 \\
+\ 9 \\
\hline
\boxed{}
\end{array}
$$

4.
$$
\begin{array}{r}
6 \\
+\ \boxed{} \\
\hline
19
\end{array}
$$

5.
$$
\begin{array}{r}
18 \\
+\ \boxed{} \\
\hline
19
\end{array}
$$

6.
$$
\begin{array}{r}
4 \\
+\ \boxed{} \\
\hline
19
\end{array}
$$

C Use 19 cubes to make 19.

Pair work

◯ + ◯ + ◯

1. **Record your answers.**

$\boxed{} + \boxed{} + \boxed{} = 19$

$\boxed{} + \boxed{} + \boxed{} = 19$

$\boxed{} + \boxed{} + \boxed{} = 19$

$\boxed{} + \boxed{} + \boxed{} = 19$

2. **Try these.**

$4 + \boxed{} + 9 = 19$

$2 + \boxed{} + 7 = 19$

$3 + \boxed{} + 7 = 19$

$8 + \boxed{} + 2 = 19$

Objectives
• Add numbers without renaming within 20.
• Develop an understanding of addition by combining or partitioning sets, use concrete materials.

Strand   Number
Strand Unit   Operations

I will learn about the number 20.

A Write the number.

20 ⟋20 ⟋20 ⟋20 ⟋20

B Draw 20 balloons in the box. Colour.

C Can you put 20 cubes into the hoops in different ways?

\+

Record your answers.

☐ + ☐ = 20	☐ + ☐ = 20	☐ + ☐ = 20
☐ + ☐ = 20	☐ + ☐ = 20	☐ + ☐ = 20
☐ + ☐ = 20	☐ + ☐ = 20	☐ + ☐ = 20

Objectives Develop an understanding of addition by combining or partitioning sets, use concrete materials.

| **Strand** | Number |
| **Strand Unit** | Operations |

I will learn about numbers that add to make 20.

Addition 20 · 53

10   10

| 1 | 2 | 3 | 4 | 5 | 6 | 7 | 8 | 9 | 10 | 11 | 12 | 13 | 14 | 15 | 16 | 17 | 18 | 19 | 20 |

$$10 + 10 = 20$$

A Use the number strip to do these.

1. $10 + 10 = \boxed{}$ 2. $8 + \boxed{} = 20$ 3. $\boxed{} + 7 = 20$

4. $4 + 16 = \boxed{}$ 5. $2 + \boxed{} = 20$ 6. $\boxed{} + 10 = 20$

7. $6 + 14 = \boxed{}$ 8. $9 + \boxed{} = 20$ 9. $\boxed{} + 5 = 20$

B Use the number strip or counters to do these.

1. $\begin{array}{r} 19 \\ +\ 1 \\ \hline \boxed{} \end{array}$ 2. $\begin{array}{r} 16 \\ +\ 4 \\ \hline \boxed{} \end{array}$ 3. $\begin{array}{r} 3 \\ +\ 17 \\ \hline \boxed{} \end{array}$ 4. $\begin{array}{r} 11 \\ +\ \boxed{} \\ \hline 20 \end{array}$ 5. $\begin{array}{r} 0 \\ +\ \boxed{} \\ \hline 20 \end{array}$ 6. $\begin{array}{r} 14 \\ +\ \boxed{} \\ \hline 20 \end{array}$

C Use 20 cubes to make 20.

Pair work

 +  +

1. **Record your answers.**

$\boxed{} + \boxed{} + \boxed{} = 20$

$\boxed{} + \boxed{} + \boxed{} = 20$

$\boxed{} + \boxed{} + \boxed{} = 20$

$\boxed{} + \boxed{} + \boxed{} = 20$

2. **Try these.**

$4 + \boxed{} + 12 = 20$

$7 + \boxed{} + 10 = 20$

$3 + \boxed{} + 7 = 20$

$5 + \boxed{} + 3 = 20$

Objectives
- Add numbers without renaming within 20.
- Develop an understanding of addition by combining or partitioning sets, use concrete materials 0–20.

Strand	Number
Strand Unit	Operations

A

1. $16 + \boxed{} = 19$

2. $11 + \boxed{} = 11$

3. Which has more corners, a square or a semi-circle?

_____

4. What time is it?

_____

5. There are $\boxed{}$ less apples than oranges.

6. $3 + 4 + 5 = \boxed{}$

7.

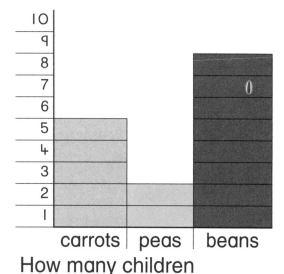

How many children liked carrots? $\boxed{}$

8. $2 + \boxed{} = 8$
$\boxed{\dfrac{}{8}}$

B

1. Write the numbers which are 3 less.

2. Circle the smallest number.

5   7   3   9   6

3. $\boxed{} + 5 = 11$

4.

Who has the most marbles? _____

5. Fill in the missing numbers.

6. $2 + 8 = \boxed{} + 5$

7. Colour the ▲. How many? $\boxed{}$

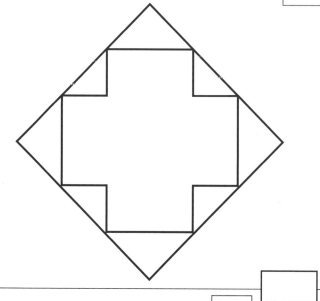

8. $3 + 7 + 4 = \boxed{}$
$\boxed{\dfrac{}{8}}$

Near doubles

Now that we know our doubles we can work on near doubles.

3 + 3 is a double,

3 + 4 is a near double so we can use our double which is

3 + 3 and then add 1.

(3 + 3) + 1 = 7

A Circle the sums that are near doubles.

3 + 4	4 + 4	4 + 5	7 + 7	8 + 9	6 + 7
3 + 3	2 + 3	8 + 9	6 + 6	5 + 6	7 + 8

B Match these.

3 + 4   4 + 4 + 1   7 + 8   2 + 2 + 1

4 + 5   5 + 5 + 1   8 + 9   7 + 7 + 1

5 + 6   3 + 3 + 1   2 + 3   8 + 8 + 1

C Write the sums below in the correct box.

doubles	near doubles
2 + 2	3 + 4

7 + 7   3 + 3   6 + 6   4 + 5   6 + 7   2 + 2   8 + 9   2 + 3   4 + 4   3 + 4   8 + 8   7 + 8   9 + 9   1 + 1

The Circus

Circus snacks

Find . Circle him green.   Find . Circle her blue.

1. How many ? ☐

2. How many  and ?

   ☐ + ☐ = ☐

3. How many ? ☐

4. **True or false?** ✔ or ✘

   There are more  than . ☐

   There are more  than . ☐

   There are 4 . ☐

   There are more  than . ☐

5. How many  and  and ?

   ☐ + ☐ + ☐ = ☐

6. How many  have a hat? ☐

7. How many  and ?

   ☐ + ☐ = ☐

8. How many  and ?

   ☐ + ☐ = ☐

9. How many  and  and ?

   ☐ + ☐ + ☐ = ☐

Find . Circle her red.

Problem Solving 3

1 **Pick 3 colours. Give each cat a different costume.**

2 **Which two dogs are the same? X them.**

I will group and count in tens and units to 20.

A Warm-up. Listen to your teacher.

1	2	3	4	5	6

B Colour 10. Draw a ring around them. The first one is done.

1.

ten	units
1	5

2.

ten	units

3.

ten	units

4.

ten	units

5.

ten	units

6.

ten	units

C Count in tens and units.

1. 14 = ☐ 1 ☐ ten + ☐ 4 ☐ units   2. 16 = ☐ ten + ☐ units

3. 17 = ☐ ten + ☐ units   4. 19 = ☐ ten + ☐ units

5. 12 = ☐ ten + ☐ units   6. 15 = ☐ ten + ☐ units

7. 18 = ☐ ten + ☐ units   8. 13 = ☐ ten + ☐ units

Place Value

I will group and count in tens and units to 20.

A **Look at the numbers. How many tens and how many units?**

15	12	18
☐ ten ☐ units	☐ ten ☐ units	☐ ten ☐ units

B **Colour 10, then draw a ring around them. The first one is done.**

1. 14 = 10 + 4

2. 11 = 10 + ☐

3. ☐ = 10 + ☐

4. ☐ = 10 + ☐

5. ☐ = 10 + ☐

6. ☐ = 10 + ☐

C **Draw beads to show the numbers.**

12	
11	
16	
10	
15	
19	

I will group and count in tens and units to 20.

A 1. **Circle the digit that represents ten.**

(a) ①5   (b) 17   (c) 10   (d) 11   (e) 12   (f) 16

2. **Circle the digit that represents units.**

(a) 1③   (b) 18   (c) 17   (d) 19   (e) 14   (f) 15

B Count the cubes.

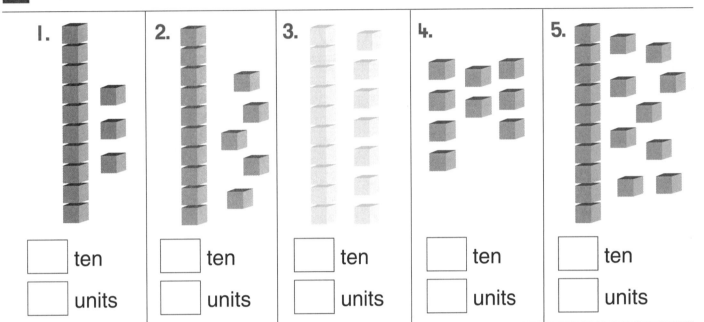

1.
[ ] ten
[ ] units

2.
[ ] ten
[ ] units

3.
[ ] ten
[ ] units

4.
[ ] ten
[ ] units

5.
[ ] ten
[ ] units

C Draw cubes to show the numbers.

1 ten 3 units	1 ten 5 units	1 ten 8 units	1 ten 4 units	2 tens

Money

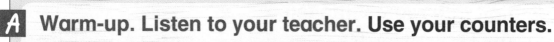
I will add up different amounts of coins.

A Warm-up. Listen to your teacher. Use your counters.

B Colour.

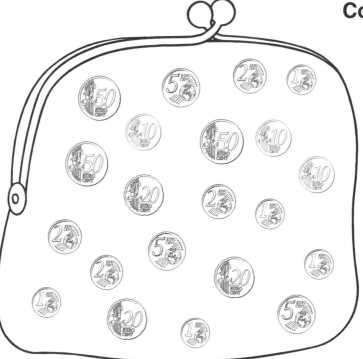

Count. How many?

C Draw the coins.

11c

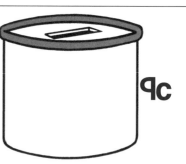
9c

17c

21c

Recognise, exchange and use coins up to the value of 50c.

Strand	Measures
Strand Unit	Money

I will add up different amounts of coins.

A Circle the correct amount.

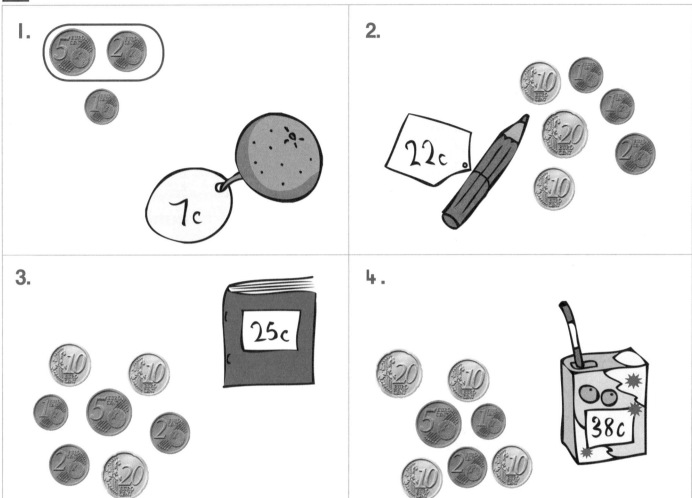

1.

7c

2.

22c

3.

25c

4.

38c

B Colour the coins you need. There is more than one answer.

18c

12c

15c

Objectives — Recognise, exchange and use coins up to the value of 50c.

Strand   Measures
Strand Unit   Money

Money

I will add up amounts and see what change I get.

A How much?

1.

☐ + ☐ = ☐ c

2.

☐ + ☐ = ☐ c

3.

☐ + ☐ = ☐ c

4.

☐ + ☐ = ☐ c

5.

☐ + ☐ = ☐ c

6.

☐ + ☐ = ☐ c

B

I have	I buy		cost	change
	7c	3c		
	8c	10c		
	6c	3c		
	 6c	10c		

C How much money in each till?

Pair work

1.

☐ c

2.

☐ c

3.

☐ c

How many stars are on the back of a coin? ☐

4.

☐ c

5.

☐ c

6.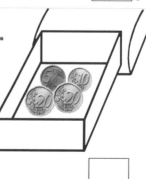

☐ c

I will add up different amounts of coins.

A Draw 2 ways to make these amounts.

1. 32c   or

2. 40c   or

3. 46c   or

4. 26c   or

5. 50c   or

B Draw the coins above the amounts.

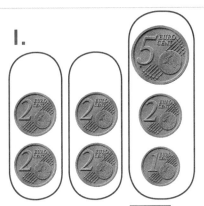
1. 4c + 4c = 8c

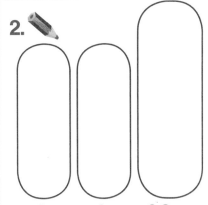
2. 12c + 8c = 20c

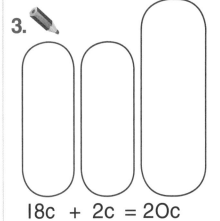
3. 18c + 2c = 20c

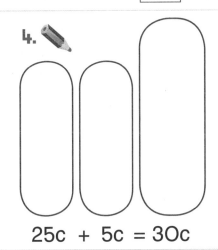
4. 25c + 5c = 30c

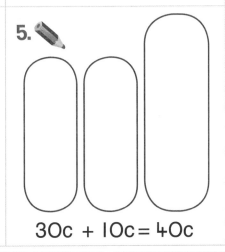
5. 30c + 10c = 40c

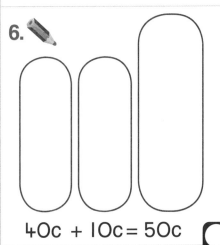
6. 40c + 10c = 50c

Objectives: Recognise, exchange and use coins up to the value of 50c.

Strand Measures
Strand Unit Money

66 Patterns

I will look at patterns.

A Warm-up. Listen to your teacher. Use your counters.

B Finish the patterns.

1.
2.
3.
4.
5.

C Pair work Finish the patterns.

D Pair work Finish the patterns.

E Draw your own pattern using shapes.

Objectives: Recognise patterns.

Strand: Algebra
Strand Unit: Extending & using patterns

I will learn about odd and even numbers.

A Which sock is the odd one out? Circle it.

B How many? Finish colouring.

How many?	odd	even
🐐	I	
🐴🐴		2
🐕🐕🐕	3	
🦆🦆🦆🦆		4
🐔🐔🐔🐔🐔		
🐑🐑		
🐥🐥🐥🐥		
🐱🐱🐱		
🐑🐑🐑		
🕊🕊🕊		

C Circle the odd numbers.

3 10 4 15 7 8 1

19 3 6 5 10 11 2

5 12 4 13 8 3 6

4 1 7 10 12 9 16

Objectives Recognise patterns including odd and even numbers.

Strand Algebra
Strand Unit Extending & using patterns

68 | Patterns

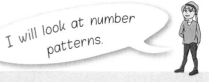

I will look at number patterns.

A Puzzle: Start at 2. Count in 2s. Colour the numbers red.
Start at 1. Count in 2s. Colour the numbers blue.

1	2	3	4	5	6	7	8	9	10
11	12	13	14	15	16	17	18	19	20
21	22	23	24	25	26	27	28	29	30
31	32	33	34	35	36	37	38	39	40
41	42	43	44	45	46	47	48	49	50
51	52	53	54	55	56	57	58	59	60
61	62	63	64	65	66	67	68	69	70
71	72	73	74	75	76	77	78	79	80
81	82	83	84	85	86	87	88	89	90
91	92	93	94	95	96	97	98	99	100

B Use the 100 grid above to help you with these.

1.

3 + 10 = ☐

13 + 10 = ☐

23 + 10 = ☐

43 + 10 = ☐

63 + 10 = ☐

2.

6 + 3 = ☐

16 + 3 = ☐

36 + 3 = ☐

56 + 3 = ☐

76 + 3 = ☐

3.

12 + 7 = ☐

22 + 7 = ☐

32 + 7 = ☐

42 + 7 = ☐

72 + 7 = ☐

4.

10 + 10 = ☐

20 + 10 = ☐

30 + 10 = ☐

50 + 10 = ☐

70 + 10 = ☐

5.

25 + 5 = ☐

35 + 5 = ☐

45 + 5 = ☐

55 + 5 = ☐

75 + 5 = ☐

6.

8 + 10 = ☐

18 + 10 = ☐

28 + 10 = ☐

68 + 10 = ☐

88 + 10 = ☐

Objectives
• Explore and use patterns in addition facts.
• Understand the use of a frame to sow the presence of an unknown number.

Strand Algebra
Strand Unit Extending & using patterns

A 1. How much?  [ ] c

2. Draw the hands to show 12 o'clock.

3. 15 = 3 + 4 + [ ]

4. 20 = 7 + [ ] + 7

5. Fill in the missing numbers.
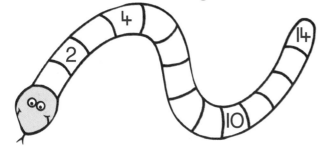

6.
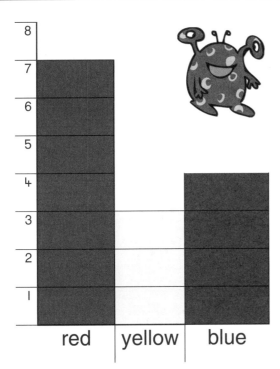

How many children liked blue and yellow? [ ]

7. 5 + [ ] = 8

8. 14c + 10c = [ ] c

[8]

B 1.

[ ] tens [ ] units

2. Circle the two numbers that make 10.

5   7   3   9   6

3. 5 + 3 = 3 + [ ]

4. Write the numbers, which are 4 more.

(3) → ( )   (8) → ( )

5.

| | May | | | | | |
M	T	W	T	F	S	S
					1	2
3	4	5	6	7	8	9
10	11	12	13	14	15	16
17	18	19	20	21	22	23
24	25	26	27	28	29	30
31						

How many Mondays in May? [ ]

6. 53 + 10 = [ ]

7. [ ] + 5 = 5 + 4

8. 16 + 3 = [ ]

[8]

Subtraction

When you take O away from a number, the number stays the same.

A

9	–	O	=	
8	–	O	=	
6	–	O	=	
7	–	O	=	
5	–	O	=	

B

9	–	O	=	
8	–	O	=	
6	–	O	=	
7	–	O	=	
10	–	O	=	

1	2	3	4	5	6	7	8	9	10
11	12	13	14	15	16	17	18	19	20
21	22	23	24	25	26	27	28	29	30
31	32	33	34	35	36	37	38	39	40
41	42	43	44	45	46	47	48	49	50
51	52	53	54	55	56	57	58	59	60
61	62	63	64	65	66	67	68	69	70
71	72	73	74	75	76	77	78	79	80
81	82	83	84	85	86	87	88	89	90
91	92	93	94	95	96	97	98	99	100

Counting backwards on the 100 square.

eg. $14 - 2 = 12$

Cover 14 with one finger then count backwards two spaces. Where did you land? 12

C Try these by counting backwards on your 100 square.

$12 - 2 =$ ☐

$10 - 2 =$ ☐

$10 - 3 =$ ☐

$16 - 2 =$ ☐

$8 - 2 =$ ☐

$15 - 4 =$ ☐

$20 - 2 =$ ☐

$10 - 3 =$ ☐

$13 - 2 =$ ☐

$19 - 2 =$ ☐

$17 \quad 3 =$ ☐

$17 - 2 =$ ☐

$16 - 2 =$ ☐

$19 - 2 =$ ☐

$15 - 2 =$ ☐

$18 - 4 =$ ☐

$11 - 2 =$ ☐

$19 - 9 =$ ☐

$20 - 1 =$ ☐

$16 - 1 =$ ☐

$17 - 1 =$ ☐

$14 - 2 =$ ☐

$13 - 3 =$ ☐

$18 - 2 =$ ☐

Riddles

1 I have no sides and no corners. What shape am I?

_____

2 I have 4 sides that are all the same size and 4 corners. What shape am I? _____

3 I have 3 sides and 3 corners. What shape am I?

_____

4 I have 4 sides, with opposite sides the same size and I have 4 corners. What shape am I?

_____

5 I am half a circle. What shape am I?

_____

6 I cannot roll. I look like a dice. What shape am I? Cube or square?_____

 Puzzle:

1. Help the rabbit get the carrot.

2. Find 2 cats the same. X them.

I will group and count in tens and units up to 20.

A Warm-up. Listen to your teacher.

1. ☐ 2. ☐ 3. ☐ 4. ☐ 5. ☐

B Match to the abacus. Write the numbers.

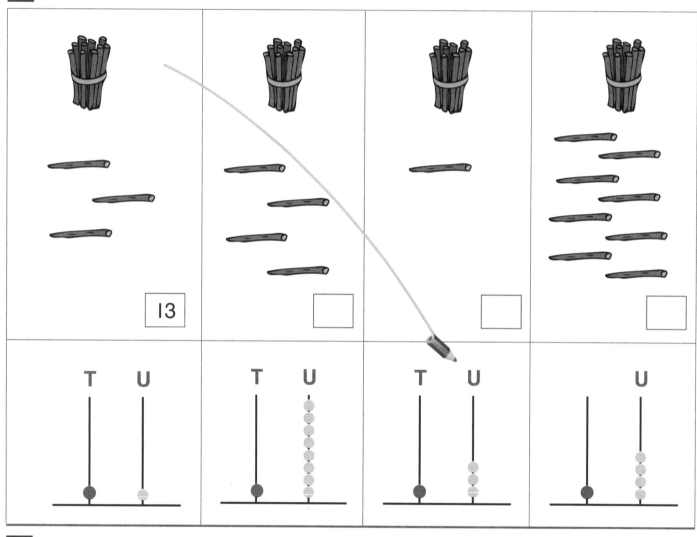

13

T U   T U   T U   U

C Write in the number on each abacus.

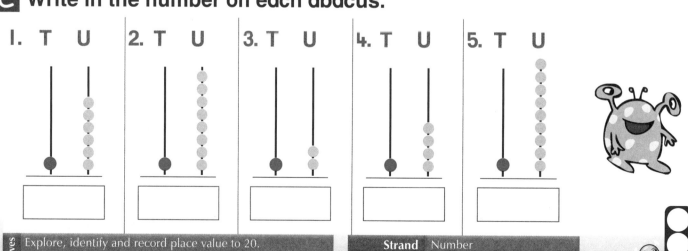

1. T U   2. T U   3. T U   4. T U   5. T U

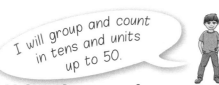

I will group and count in tens and units up to 50.

A Write the number.

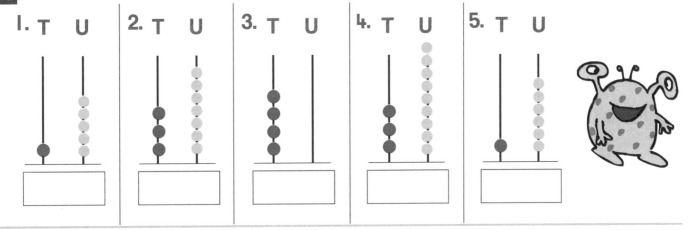

1. T U	2. T U	3. T U	4. T U	5. T U

B Circle the tens. Write the numbers.

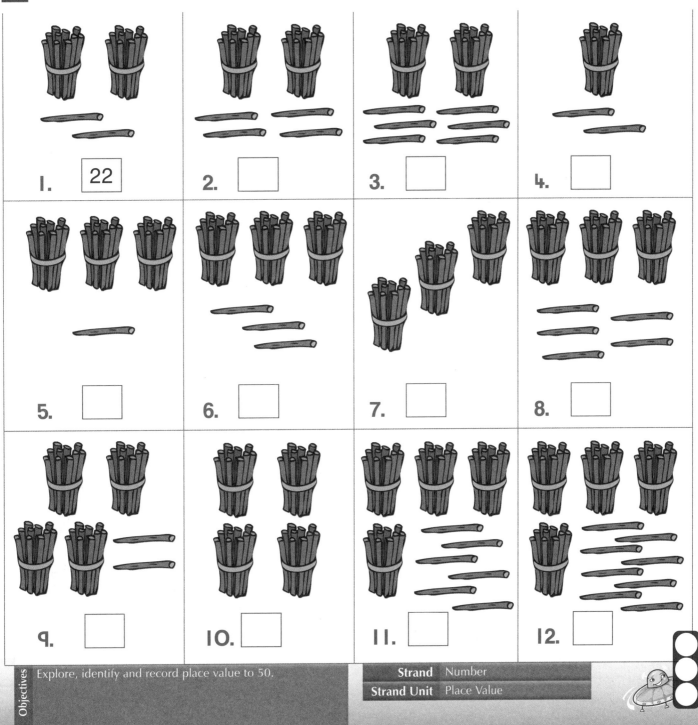

1. | 22 |

2.

3.

4.

5.

6.

7.

8.

9.

10.

11.

12.

My goal is to group and count in tens and units up to 50.

A 1. **Circle the digit that represents tens.**

(a) 2③   (b) 35   (c) 3⑨   (d) 42   (e) 50

2. **Circle the digit that represents units.**

(a) 2⑨   (b) 31   (c) 44   (d) 48   (e) 50

B How many cubes?

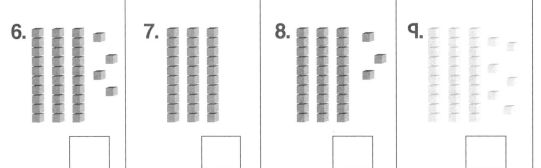

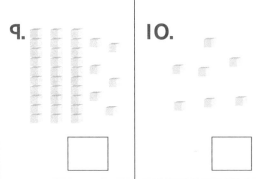

1. ☐ 12

2. ☐

3. ☐

4. ☐

5. ☐

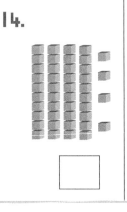
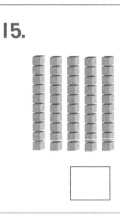

6. ☐

7. ☐

8. ☐

9. ☐

10. ☐

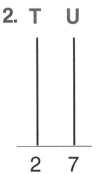
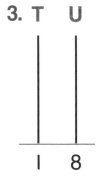
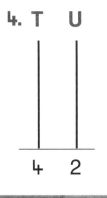
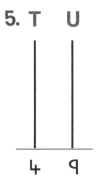

11. ☐

12. ☐

13. ☐

14. ☐

15. ☐

C Draw dots to show each number on the abacus.

1. T U   2. T U   3. T U   4. T U   5. T U

1 3   2 7   1 8   4 2   4 9

Objectives Explore, identify and record place value to 50.

Strand	Number
Strand Unit	Place Value

I will learn about long and short.

A Warm-up. Listen to your teacher.

   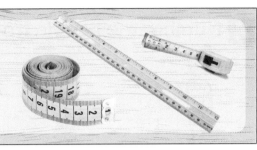

B Colour the longer object in each pair.

1.

2.

3.

4.

C Colour the shorter object in each pair.

1.

2.

3.

4.

D Colour the tallest person red. Colour the shortest person blue.

 Pair work

1. Who is the tallest? _____   2. Who is the shortest? _____

Seán   Tom   Mark   Mary   Ann   Tara

Objectives Estimate, compare, measure and record length using non-standard units.

Strand	Measures
Strand Unit	Length

I will learn new words like 'tall' and 'low'.

A Number the people from the tallest to the shortest.

 1   □  □  □  □

B Colour the:

tallest	
highest	
longest	
shortest	
lowest	

C Draw.

Draw a lower wall.		
Draw a smaller house.		
Draw a shorter brush.		

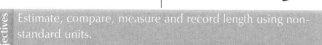
Objectives Estimate, compare, measure and record length using non-standard units.

Strand   Measures
Strand Unit   Length

A Measure these things using a cube  and a pencil.

	with a		with a	
	estimate	measure	estimate	measure
length of this page				
width of this page				
length of my desk				

B Fill in the words longer, shorter, taller.

1. A girl is _____ than a house.
2. My table is _____ than my book.
3. A car is _____ than a bus.
4. My hand is _____ than my arm.

C Pair work   Measure lengths around you.

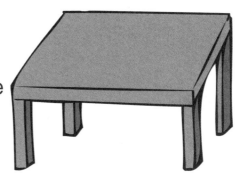

1. The table is _____ books wide or _____ hand spans wide.

2. The window is _____ books wide or _____ hand spans wide.

3. The bookcase is _____ books wide or _____ hand spans wide.

Objectives
• Estimate, compare, measure and record length using non-standard units.
• Select and use non-standard measuring units and instruments.

Strand   Measures
Strand Unit   Length

I will use a metre stick.

A Pair work **Use a metre stick or string to measure.**

along the whiteboard	across your table	
across the window	across the door	width of the classroom

Remember: A metre is always the same length as another metre.

B Pair work **Measure around the school. Use a metre stick or string.**

	our estimate	length
width of front door of school		
length of playground		
width of playground		

C Estimate first and then measure these at home. Use a ruler or string.

	estimate	measure
length of bedroom	___ metres	___ metres
width of bedroom	___ metres	___ metres
length of sitting room	___ metres	___ metres

Objectives Estimate, measure and record length using standard unit (the metre).

Strand Measures
Strand Unit Length

I will follow directions.

A Warm-up. Listen to your teacher. Tick the correct box.

left ☐   underneath ☐   through ☐   on top of ☐

right ☐   between ☐   around ☐

B Draw.

1. A cat underneath the tree.

2. A bird on top of the tree.

3. A boy to the left of the tree.

4. A dog to the right of the tree.

5. A turtle between the tree and the boy.

6. A tree to the right of the dog.

7. A rabbit going through the two trees.

8. A scarf around the boy's neck.

C Help the dragon to get the flower.

Pair work

Objectives Explore, discuss, develop and use the vocabulary of spatial relations.

Strand	Shape and Space
Strand Unit	Spatial Awareness

I will use direction words.

A Help the artist to finish colouring the picture.

True or false? ✓ or ×.

1. The 🚂 is on the left side of the picture. ☐

2. The 🐱 is on top of the 🎒. ☐

3. The 🥔 is on top of the 🚂. ☐

4. 🧒 is between the 🪣 and the cow. ☐

B In your copy, draw something:

1. to the left of you. 2. in front of you.

3. to the right of you. 4. behind you.

Objectives — Explore, discuss, develop and use the vocabulary of spatial relations.

Strand Shape and Space
Strand Unit Spatial Awareness

I will learn about doubles.

A Match the number to the correct word.

4   10   1   7   8   2   9   3   6   5

one   two   three   four   five   six   seven   eight   nine   ten

B Match the correct balloon to the ribbon. Colour them the same.

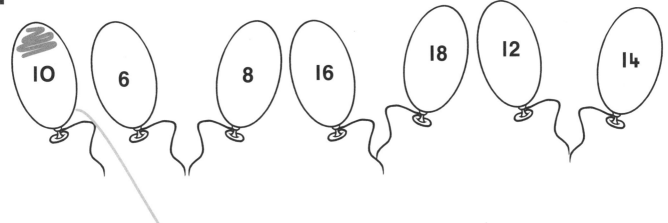

10   6   8   16   18   12   14

4 + 4   3 + 3   5 + 5   9 + 9   6 + 6   8 + 8   7 + 7

C Fill in the answers.

1. 3 + 3 = ☐

2. 6 + 6 = ☐

3. 7 + 7 = ☐

4. 8 + 8 = ☐

5. 4 + 4 = ☐

6. 2 + 2 = ☐

D Try these.

1. ☐ + 9 = 18

2. ☐ + 5 = 10

3. 6 + ☐ = 12

4. 7 + ☐ = 14

5. ☐ + 8 = 16

6. ☐ + 10 = 20

Objectives: Develop and/or recall mental strategies for addition facts within 20.

Strand   Number
Strand Unit   Addition

Addition

I will learn near doubles.

A Match the rabbit to the correct carrot.

B Try these.

1. $1 + 1 =$ ☐ SO $1 + 2 =$ ☐

2. $5 + 5 =$ ☐ SO $5 + 6 =$ ☐

3. $7 + 7 =$ ☐ SO $7 + 8 =$ ☐

4. $4 + 4 =$ ☐ SO $4 + 5 =$ ☐

5. $6 + 6 =$ ☐ SO $6 + 7 =$ ☐

6. $8 + 8 =$ ☐ SO $8 + 9 =$ ☐

Objectives: Develop and/or recall mental strategies for addition facts within 20.

Strand	Number
Strand Unit	Addition

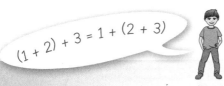

$(1 + 2) + 3 = 1 + (2 + 3)$

(1 + 2) + 3 = 6

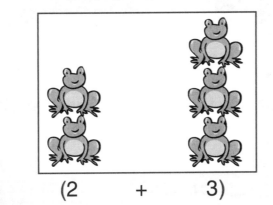 

1 + (2 + 3) = 6

A Try these.

1. (2 + 1) + 3 = ☐ and 2 + (1 + 3) = ☐

2. (4 + 3) + 1 = ☐ and 4 + (3 + 1) = ☐

3. (1 + 5) + 2 = ☐ and 1 + (5 + 2) = ☐

4. (6 + 3) + 1 = ☐ and 6 + (3 + 1) = ☐

5. (7 + 4) + 2 = ☐ and 7 + (4 + 2) = ☐

6. (8 + 3) + 4 = ☐ and 8 + (3 + 4) = ☐

Objectives: Explore, develop and apply the associative property of addition.

Strand: Number
Strand Unit: Addition

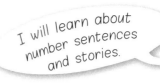

I will learn about number sentences and stories.

A **Write a number sentence for these pictures.**

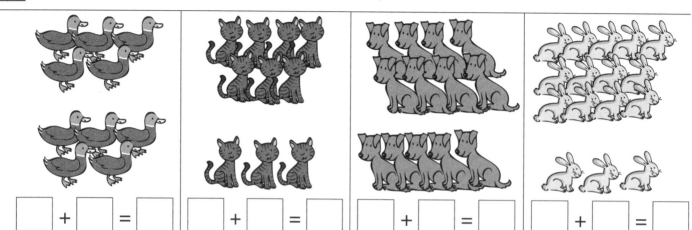

☐ + ☐ = ☐   ☐ + ☐ = ☐   ☐ + ☐ = ☐   ☐ + ☐ = ☐

B **Match the correct picture to the correct number sentence.**

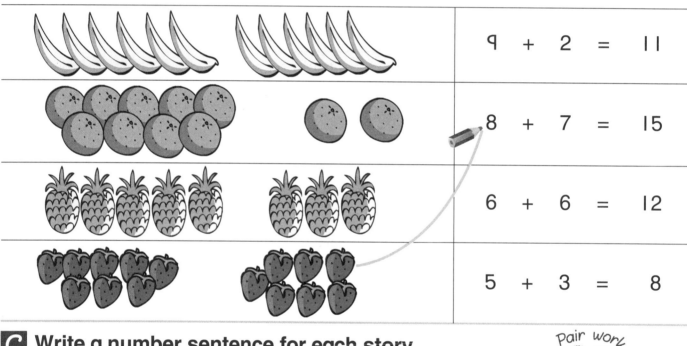

9 + 2 = 11

8 + 7 = 15

6 + 6 = 12

5 + 3 = 8

C **Write a number sentence for each story.**

Pair work

1. Sam had 5 apples and Mary had 2 apples. How many apples did they have **altogether**?

   5 + ☐ = 7

2. Peter had 6 sweets and Jack had 3 sweets. How many sweets had they **both** got?   ☐ + ☐ = ☐

3. Josh had 7 books on loan from the library. Ben had 3 books on loan from the library. How many books had Josh **and** Ben on loan from the library?   ☐ + ☐ = ☐

Objectives
• Construct number sentences and number stories.
• Solve problems involving addition within 20.

Strand	Number
Strand Unit	Addition

I will learn about number sentences.

A Fill in the missing numbers.

1.

| 3 | + | 7 | = | 10 |

2.

| 6 | + | | = | |

3.

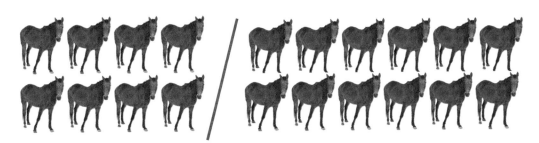

| | + | | = | |

4.

| | + | | = | |

5.

| | + | | = | |

A

1. Finish the pattern.

2. Circle the odd numbers.

6   3   1   7   2

3. $23 + 10 =$ ☐

4. What time is it?

  _____ o'clock

5. How much?

      ☐ c

6. Put a ring around the longest pencil.

7. Fill in the missing numbers.

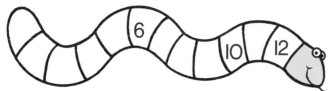

8.

Circle the tallest.   ☐/8

B

1. Eileen had 7 marbles. Rita had 6 marbles. How many had they altogether? ☐

2. Circle all the even numbers.

2   5   3   4   8

3.

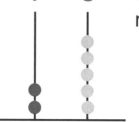

What is the number? ☐

4. How many hand spans wide is your table? ☐

5.

Draw a bucket on the left of the red rug.

6. $3 + 5 =$ ☐ $+ 3$

7. Tony had 9 sweets. Ronan had the same. How many had they altogether? ☐

8. $(2 + 4) + 3 =$ ☐

☐/8

Subtraction. Counting backwards.

1	2	3	4	5	6	7	8	9	10
11	12	13	14	15	16	17	18	19	20

When you subtract 3 from a number, you move back 3 spaces. Test yourself, then check your answers. Try these.

A

3	−	3	=	0
4	−	3	=	
5	−	3	=	
6	−	3	=	
7	−	3	=	
8	−	3	=	
9	−	3	=	
10	−	3	=	
11	−	3	=	
12	−	3	=	

B

11	−	3	=	
12	−	3	=	
13	−	3	=	
14	−	3	=	
15	−	3	=	
16	−	3	=	
17	−	3	=	
18	−	3	=	
19	−	3	=	
20	−	3	=	

1	2	3	4	5	6	7	8	9	10
11	12	13	14	15	16	17	18	19	20
21	22	23	24	25	26	27	28	29	30
31	32	33	34	35	36	37	38	39	40

C Now try with bigger numbers.

38	−	3	=	35
23	−	3	=	
34	−	3	=	
26	−	3	=	
27	−	3	=	

D

22	−	3	=	
30	−	3	=	
29	−	3	=	
40	−	3	=	
39	−	3	=	
31	−	3	=	

Game. When you land on the following, it means:

Go forward 1 space

Roll again

Go forward 2 spaces

Go back 1 space

You must roll the exact number to win!

Start Roll the Dice.

Great Deals! Super Savings!

15c

20c

30c

25c

1. How much is an 🍎 and an 🍏? ☐

2. How much is 2 🍎? ☐

3. Sean bought a 🍌 and a 🍐. How much change did he get from 50c? ☐

4. Susan has two 10c coins. How much more does she need to buy a banana? ☐

1

2

4

5

9

10

5. Write the shape of each of the following foods.

cuboid   cylinder   sphere

6. How many eggs are missing from the tray? ☐

7. The yellow apples are on the _____ of the green apples. right left

8. The red apples are on the _____ of the green apples. right left

9. Closing time is 6 o'clock.
Show 6 o'clock.

Finish 30

28

26

24

23

20

 13 **15** **16** **18**

Problem Solving 5

Target board

A row goes across. A column goes down.

8	12	19
22	24	7
33	42	14
85	9	63
66	54	25

1 How many rows and columns can you count?

rows ☐   columns ☐

2 In your copy, add 10 to each number. Show it as a sum.

e.g. 8 + 10 = 18

3 How many odd numbers in the first column?

☐

4 How many even numbers in the fifth row?

☐

5 Can you find 4 pairs of socks for the octopus?

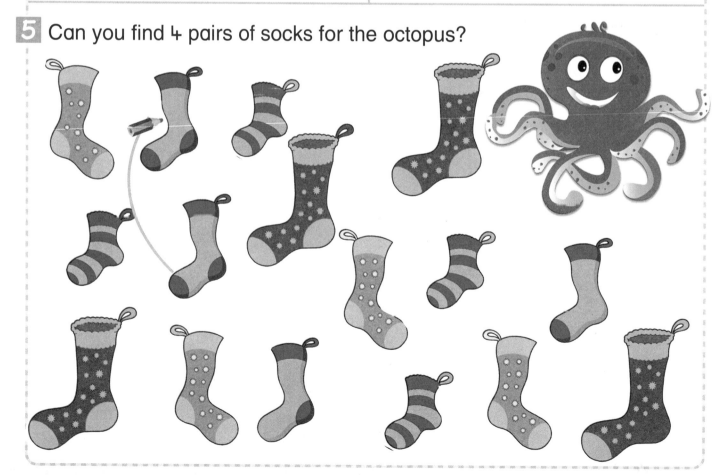

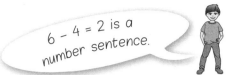

6 – 4 = 2 is a number sentence.

A **Colour the ducks that are left. Write the number sentences in two ways.**

1.	7 – 2 = 5	7 – 2 5
2.	6 – 4 = ☐	☐ – ☐
3.	8 – ☐ = ☐	☐ – ☐
4.	☐ – ☐ = ☐	☐ – ☐

B **In your copy, draw your own pictures for these number sentences.**

1. 6 – 2 = 4

2. 8 – 5 = 3

3. 9 – 4 = 5

4. 5 – 3 = 2

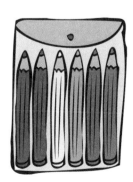

C **Puzzle: Colour by number.**

2	3	4	5

8 – 3   9 – 5

7
– 5

4 – 1   7 – 2

Objectives
• Develop an understanding of subtraction as deducting.
• Record subtraction pictorially.

Strand Number
Strand Unit Subtraction

Subtraction

I will write number sentences.

A Warm-up. Listen to your teacher.

B Try these.

1.

How many birds were there? ☐

How many flew away? ☐

How many are left? ☐

9 – ☐ = 7

2.

How many birds were there? ☐

How many flew away? ☐

How many are left? ☐

☐ – ☐ = ☐

3.

How many birds were there? ☐

How many flew away? ☐

How many are left? ☐

☐ – ☐ = ☐

C Try these.

1.

☐ – ☐ = ☐

2.

☐ – ☐ = ☐

D Draw a bird picture.

$7 - 3 = 4$

Objectives Develop an understanding of subtraction as deducting.

Strand	Number
Strand Unit	Subtraction

I will learn about light and heavy things.

A Warm-up. Listen to your teacher.

B Circle the heavy things red. Circle the light things blue.

C Write lighter or heavier.

1. A  is _____ than a  .

2. A is _____ than a  .

3. A  is _____ than a .

4. An is _____ than a .

D Draw something heavier than:

E Puzzle: Draw 2 things that you think are about the same weight as this book.

Objectives: Estimate, compare, measure and record weight using non-standard units.

Strand   Measures
Strand Unit   Weight

Weight

When things balance, they weigh the same.

A Who weighs the same?

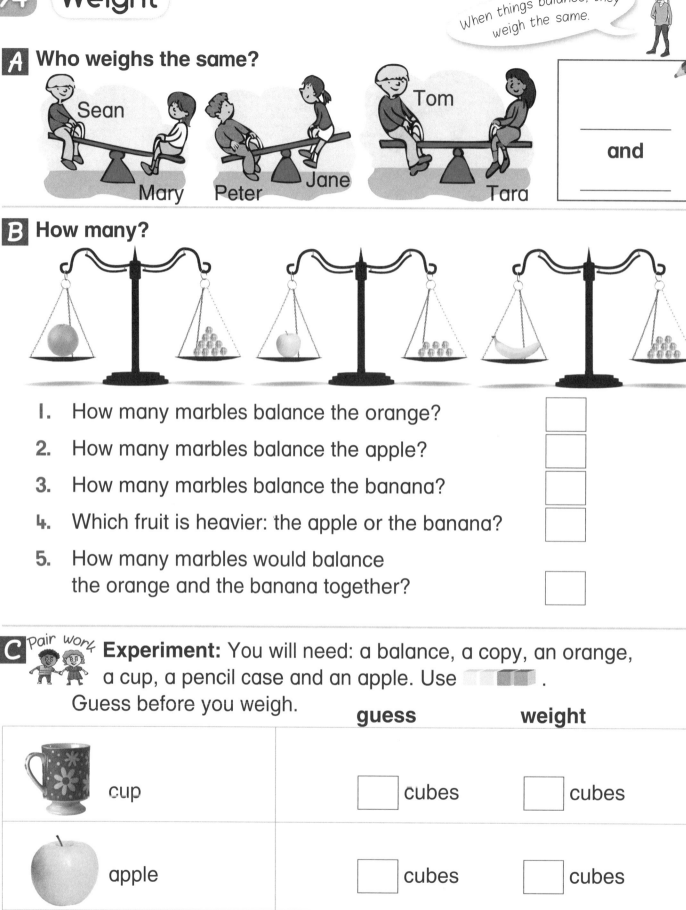

Sean Mary Peter Jane Tom Tara

_____ and _____

B How many?

1. How many marbles balance the orange?
2. How many marbles balance the apple?
3. How many marbles balance the banana?
4. Which fruit is heavier: the apple or the banana?
5. How many marbles would balance the orange and the banana together?

C Pair work

Experiment: You will need: a balance, a copy, an orange, a cup, a pencil case and an apple. Use ▭▮. Guess before you weigh.

	guess	weight
cup	☐ cubes	☐ cubes
apple	☐ cubes	☐ cubes
pencil case	☐ cubes	☐ cubes

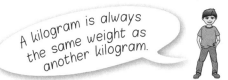

A kilogram is always the same weight as another kilogram.

A Sean the shopkeeper used a scales. He put a 1 kilogram weight on one side.

1. How many apples weigh the same as 1kg? ☐

2. How many oranges weigh the same as 1kg? ☐

3. How many bananas weigh the same as 1kg? ☐

4. Which fruit is heavier: an apple or a banana? ☐

5. Which fruit is lighter: an apple or an orange? ☐

B *Pair work* You will need a scales and a kilogram weight (or a bag of sugar).

Estimate how many of each object would weigh 1kg.

	estimate	result	difference
copy			
maths book			

C Puzzle:

1. Which is heavier: 1kg of coal or 1kg of feathers?
2. Which is heavier: A bag of coal or a bag of groceries?

Answers: 1. They are the same weight!
2. It depends on the size of the bag!

Objectives Estimate, measure and record weight using standard unit (the kilogramme) and solve simple problems.

Strand Measures
Strand Unit Weight

Weight

I will use kilograms to measure weight.

A What weighs the same?

6 potatoes weigh ☐ kilogram.

1 cabbage weighs ☐ kilogram.

☐ carrots weigh 1 kilogram.

B Pair work What do you think? Circle the items heavier than 1kg red. Circle the items lighter than 1kg blue.

C At home: Use a scales to find the weight. ☐ the box.

	about 1kg	heavier than 1kg	lighter than 1kg

Objectives Estimate, measure and record weight, using standard unit (the kilogramme) and solve simple problems.

Strand Measures
Strand Unit Weight

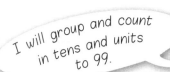

I will group and count in tens and units to 99.

A Write T (tens) or U (units) to show the circled digit.

1. (5)8 ☐   2. 6(0) ☐   3. (7)7 ☐   4. (9)4 ☐   5. 8(3) ☐

B Count the sticks.

1. 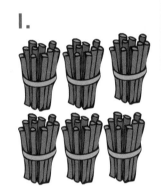 ☐

2.  ☐

3.  ☐

4.  ☐

5. 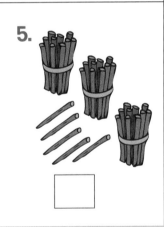 ☐

6. 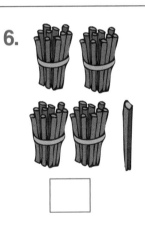 ☐

7.  ☐

8.  ☐

C Draw beads to show the numbers on the abacus.

1. T U   2. T U   3. T U   4. T U   5. T U

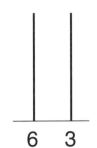 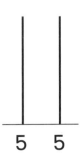 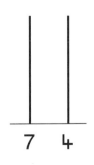 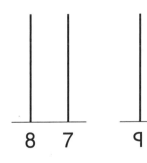 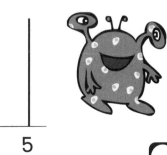

6 3   5 5   7 4   8 7   9 5

I will group and count in tens and units to 99.

A 1. **Circle the numeral that means tens.**

(a) 45   (b) 53   (c) 62   (d) 71   (e) 88

2. **Circle the numeral that means units.**

(a) 59   (b) 68   (c) 84   (d) 79   (e) 93

B Draw the cubes.

1. 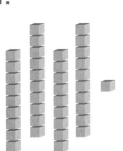 41	2. 57	3. 32	4. 61
5. 75	6. 84	7. 89	8. 96

C Draw beads to show the numbers on the abacus.

1. T U   2. T U   3. T U   4. T U   5. T U

6   2   4   8   7   9   9   2   5   7

Objectives   Explore, identify and record place value 0–99.

Strand	Number
Strand Unit	Place Value

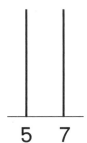

I will write number sentences.

A. Fill in the missing numbers on the number line.

0   1   ☐   3   ☐   5   6   ☐   8   ☐   10

B.

6 birds were on a line.

2 birds flew away.

How many are left?

$6 - 2 = $ ☐

C. Finish these number sentences.

1. $5 - 3 = $ ☐

2. $7 - 4 = $ ☐

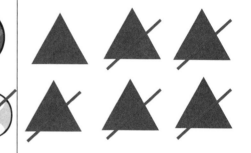

3. $6 - 5 = $ ☐

4. $8 - 3 = $ ☐

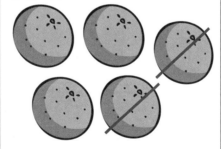

5. $5 - 2 = $ ☐

6. $7 - 3 = $ ☐

D. Try these. Use counters.

1. $8 - 2 = $ ☐   2. $7 - 5 = $ ☐   3. $9 - 4 = $ ☐

4. $6 - 4 = $ ☐   5. $8 - 3 = $ ☐   6. $5 - 3 = $ ☐

7. $9 - 3 = $ ☐   8. $6 - 5 = $ ☐   9. $8 - 5 = $ ☐

Objectives
• Develop an understanding of subtraction as deducting.
• Record subtraction in number sentences.

Strand	Number
Strand Unit	Subtraction

Subtraction

I will write number sentences.

9 ducks were on a pond.
4 flew away. 5 stayed.
9 − 4 = 5

A Finish each number sentence. Cross off the things you take away.
Colour the things that are left over.

1. 5 − 3 = ☐

2. 6 − 2 = ☐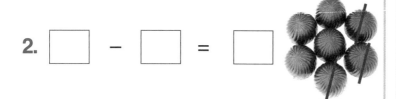

3. 7 − 4 = ☐

4. 8 − 3 = ☐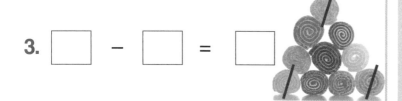

B Write your own number sentence.

C Puzzle: Colour by number.

4	2
3	5

1. ☐ − ☐ = ☐

2. ☐ − ☐ = ☐

3. ☐ − ☐ = ☐

4. ☐ − ☐ = ☐

5 − 3   8 − 5   6 − 3

6 − 2   9 − 4   7 − 2

8 − 3   7 − 3   4 − 2

Objectives
• Develop an understanding of subtraction as deducting.
• Record subtraction pictorially.

Strand   Number
Strand Unit   Subtraction

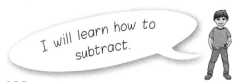

I will learn how to subtract.

A Warm-up.

$7 - 5 =$ ☐ $4 - 3 =$ ☐ $5 - 4 =$ ☐ $6 - 4 =$ ☐ $8 - 1 =$ ☐

B As quickly as you can, draw lines to join the cats and kittens.

C Try these. Use counters.

1. $8 - 3 =$ ☐
2. $8 - 5 =$ ☐
3. $9 - 2 =$ ☐
4. $9 - 4 =$ ☐
5. $8 - 6 =$ ☐
6. $7 - 7 =$ ☐
7. $7 - 4 =$ ☐
8. $6 - 4 =$ ☐
9. $6 - 2 =$ ☐
10. $8 - 7 =$ ☐

D Puzzle: Can you spot 5 differences?

E

1. $\begin{array}{r} 6 \\ -3 \\ \hline \end{array}$
2. $\begin{array}{r} 8 \\ -5 \\ \hline \end{array}$
3. $\begin{array}{r} 9 \\ -4 \\ \hline \end{array}$
4. $\begin{array}{r} 8 \\ -6 \\ \hline \end{array}$

5. $\begin{array}{r} 7 \\ -5 \\ \hline \end{array}$
6. $\begin{array}{r} 9 \\ -5 \\ \hline \end{array}$
7. $\begin{array}{r} 10 \\ -3 \\ \hline \end{array}$
8. $\begin{array}{r} 10 \\ -6 \\ \hline \end{array}$

9. $\begin{array}{r} 7 \\ -4 \\ \hline \end{array}$
10. $\begin{array}{r} 9 \\ -7 \\ \hline \end{array}$
11. $\begin{array}{r} 8 \\ -4 \\ \hline \end{array}$
12. $\begin{array}{r} 10 \\ -2 \\ \hline \end{array}$

| Number Sentences

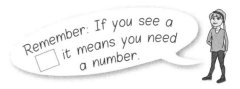

A Write the missing numbers.

$2 + \boxed{} = 4$ $3 + \boxed{} = 5$ $2 + \boxed{} = 2$

B Try these.

1. $2 + \boxed{} = 5$ 2. $3 + \boxed{} = 6$ 3. $\boxed{} + 2 = 10$

4. $3 + \boxed{} = 7$ 5. $4 + \boxed{} = 9$ 6. $\boxed{} + 4 = 10$

7. $4 + \boxed{} = 6$ 8. $5 + \boxed{} = 8$ 9. $\boxed{} + 3 = 10$

10. $5 + \boxed{} = 9$ 11. $6 + \boxed{} = 9$ 12. $\boxed{} + 1 = 10$

13. $6 + \boxed{} = 8$ 14. $3 + \boxed{} = 8$ 15. $\boxed{} + 5 = 10$

C Try these. You can use counters or cubes.

1. Anna has **6** apples. How many more does she need to have **10** apples? ☐

2. Ben has **5** cars. How many more does he need to have **10** cars? ☐

3. Sarah has **4** balloons. How many more does she need to have **6** balloons? ☐

4. Josh has **2** oranges. How many more does he need to have **8** oranges? ☐

5. Katie has **2** pencils. How many more does she need to have **9** pencils? ☐

D **Puzzle: Can you spot 5 differences? Mark them with an X.**

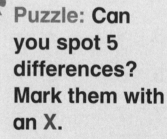

I will use words that describe where things are.

A Circle the correct answer.

1. The letter [A] is on the **right/left** side of the box.

2. The letter [B] is **underneath/on top** of the box.

3. The letter [C] is **inside/outside** the box.

4. The letter [D] is on the **right/left** side of the box.

5. Draw a pear **underneath** the box.

6. Draw an apple **on top of** the box.

B

C Help the chick to find its mammy.

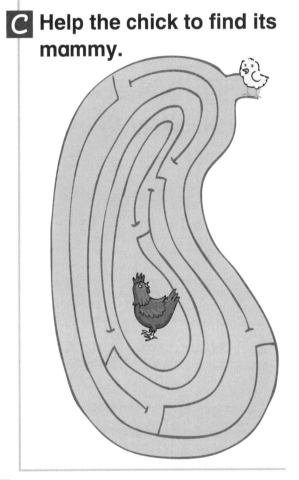

1. What is above the turtle? _____

2. What is below the bird? _____

3. What is between the horse and the elephant? _____

4. What is to the right of the cat? _____

5. What is to the left of the turtle? _____

Objectives Explore, discuss, develop and use the vocabulary of spatial relations.

Strand Shape and Space

Strand Unit Spatial Awareness

Capacity

I will guess, compare, measure and record how much or how little.

A Colour the containers that hold the most and least in each box.

B You will need:

	estimate	actual
1. How many to fill the ?		
2. How many to fill the ?		
3. How many to fill the ?		
4. How many to fill the ?		

Objectives: Estimate, compare, measure and record capacity using non-standard units.

Strand	Measures
Strand Unit	Capacity

I will answer questions about the litre.

A Tick the litre containers.

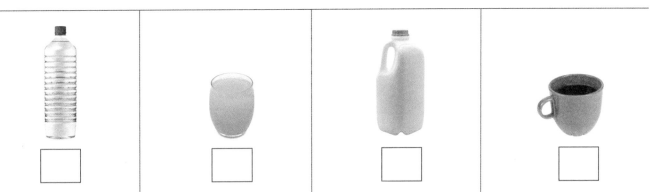

☐   ☐   ☐   ☐

B True or false? ✓ or X.

1. Milk is measured in litres.   ☐

2. All litre bottles look the same.   ☐

3. Only liquid is measured in litres.   ☐

4. All 1 litre bottles hold the same amount of liquid.   ☐

5. Sugar is measured in litres.   ☐

6. There are 1,000ml in a litre.   ☐

C Estimate, then count how many are needed to fill a litre container. You will need:

object	estimate	how many?
jar		
glass		
egg cup		
cup		

Strand	Measures
Strand Unit	Capacity

Capacity

A Tick the one that holds less.

B Draw 3 things that:

hold more than 1 litre	hold less than 1 litre	hold about the same as 1 litre
1.	1.	1.
2.	2.	2.
3.	3.	3.

C Pair work

You will need: An litre bottle of water and a glass.

1. How many glasses did you pour before the bottle was empty?

2. In your copy, draw the number of glasses you would need to fill the bottle to half full.

Objectives: Estimate, measure and record capacity using standard unit (the litre) and solve problems.

Strand	Measures
Strand Unit	Capacity

A 1. Show **25** on the abacus.

2.

3. Draw hands to show 5 o'clock.

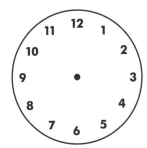 

4. 13 − 5 = ☐

Is it 10, 18 or 8?

5. 27 = 2 tens and ☐ units.

6. How much for four lollies?

 ☐ c

7. Write the numbers from lowest to highest.

70   40   90   20

☐ ☐ ☐ ☐

8. 3 + 6 + 4 = ☐

8

B 1. Colour the **third** cat.

2. Circle the coins that add up to 20c.

3. 9 − ☐ = 4

4. ▭ = 1 birthday. How many birthdays were in May?

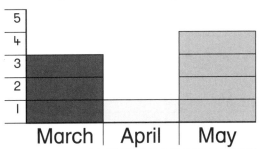

	March	April	May

5. A copy weighs:

less than 1 kg. ☐

more than 1 kg. ☐

6. The pencil weighs the same as ☐ cubes.

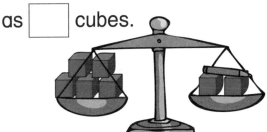

7. Ring the odd numbers.

13   14   15   16   17

8. How many days in two weeks? ☐

8

Tables

Addition

| 0 | 1 | 2 | 3 | 4 | 5 | 6 | 7 | 8 | 9 | 10 | 11 | 12 | 13 | 14 | 15 | 16 | 17 | 18 | 19 | 20 |

When you **add**, you **move forwards** on the number line.

Test yourself. Then check your answers.

A

1	+	4	=
2	+	3	=
3	+	5	=
4	+	2	=
5	+	4	=
6	+	3	=
7	+	2	=
8	+	2	=
9	+	3	=
10	+	4	=

B

11	+	3	=
12	+	4	=
13	+	2	=
14	+	5	=
15	+	2	=
16	+	3	=
17	+	2	=
18	+	0	=
19	+	1	=
20	+	0	=

1	2	3	4	5	6	7	8	9	10
11	12	13	14	15	16	17	18	19	20
21	22	23	24	25	26	27	28	29	30
31	32	33	34	35	36	37	38	39	40

C Now try with bigger numbers.

11	+	5	=
23	+	4	=
34	+	5	=
26	+	6	=
37	+	2	=

D Try both ways.

5	+	30	=
29	+	4	=
8	+	20	=
19	+	7	=
9	+	11	=

1 Colour the odd numbers green and the even numbers red.

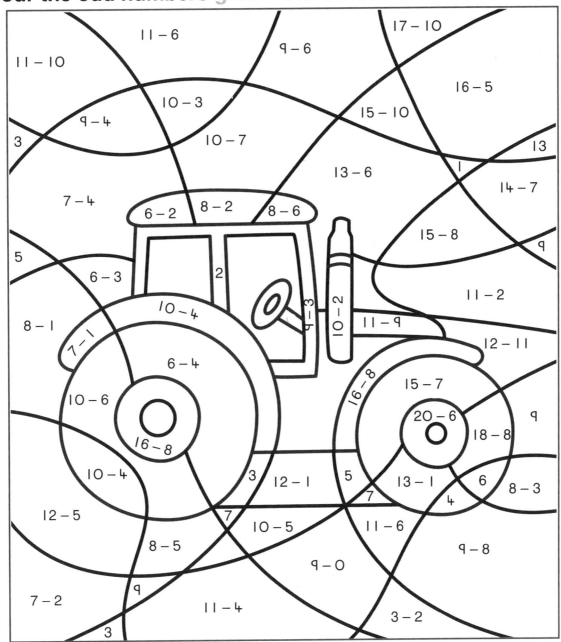

11 − 6   9 − 6   17 − 10
11 − 10   16 − 5
10 − 3   15 − 10
9 − 4   13
3   10 − 7   1   14 − 7
13 − 6
7 − 4   15 − 8
6 − 2   8 − 2   8 − 6   9
5   15 − 8
6 − 3   2   11 − 2
8 − 1   10 − 4   9 − 3   10 − 2   11 − 9   12 − 11
7 − 1
6 − 4   16 − 8   15 − 7
10 − 6   20 − 6   9
16 − 8   18 − 8
10 − 4   3   12 − 1   5   13 − 1   6   8 − 3
7   4
12 − 5   7   10 − 5   11 − 6   9 − 8
8 − 5   9 − 0
7 − 2   9   3 − 2
3   11 − 4

2 Colour the other half in the same colours.

I will learn about a 100 square.

A Fill in the gaps.

1. 16 ☐ 18 ☐ ☐ 21 ☐
2. 36 ☐ ☐ 39 ☐ ☐ 42
3. 66 ☐ ☐ ☐ 70 ☐
4. ☐ ☐ ☐ 89 90 ☐

B Hundred square fun

1	2	3	4	5	6	7	8	9	10
11	12	13	14	15	16	17	18	19	20
21	22	23	24	25	26	27	28	29	30
31	32	33	34	35	36	37	38	39	40
41	42	43	44	45	46	47	48	49	50
51	52	53	54	55	56	57	58	59	60
61	62	63	64	65	66	67	68	69	70
71	72	73	74	75	76	77	78	79	80
81	82	83	84	85	86	87	88	89	90
91	92	93	94	95	96	97	98	99	100

1. Colour all the numbers with **0** in the units place red.
2. Colour all the numbers with **7** in the units place blue.
3. Colour all the numbers with **2** in the units place green.
4. Colour all the numbers with **3** in the units place yellow.
5. Colour all the numbers with **6** in the units place purple.

C Circle the:

tens	③7
tens	79
units	52
units	13
tens	26
unit	91
tens	23
tens	44
units	85
units	68

D These are parts of the 100 square. Fill in the missing numbers.

Pair work

14

☐ 32 ☐ 34

22 23
32

45

46 47
☐ 55 ☐

67

6

24 ☐ 27

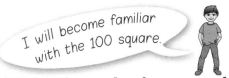

I will become familiar with the 100 square.

A Fill in the missing numbers.

1. 31 ___ ___ ___ 35   2. 24 ___ ___ ___   3. 46 ___ 48 ___ ___

4. ___ 66 ___ ___ 69   5. ___ ___ 75 76   6. ___ 97 ___ ___ 100

B What are the numbers?

1	2	3	4	5	6	7	8		10
11	12	13	14	15	16	17	18	19	20
	22	23	24	25	26	27	28	29	30
31	32	33	34	35	36	37	38	39	40
41	42	43	44	45	46	47	48		50
51	52	53	54		56	57	58	59	60
61	62	63	64	65	66	67	68	69	70
71	72		74	75	76		78	79	80
81	82	83	84	85	86	87	88	89	90
91	92	93	94		96	97	98	99	100

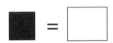 = ☐   ■ = ☐

 = ☐   ■ = ☐

 = ☐   ■ = ☐

☐ = ☐

C Try these. Use the 100 square to help you.

Pair work

1. Philip has **50** marbles. Tony has **half** this number. How many marbles has Tony? ☐

2. Amy collected **64** tokens. Her gran collected **14** for her. How many has Amy now? ☐

3. Trish needs **15c** more to buy a pencil. She already has **15c**. How much does the pencil cost? ☐ c

4. Shane has **double** the number of cards that William has. If William has **40**, how many has Shane? ☐

D Fill in the missing numbers.

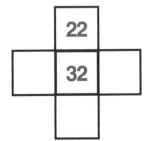

22
32

67 68

27

75

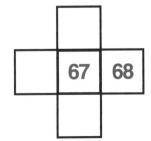

Addition

I will learn number patterns by counting.

A Warm-up. Listen to your teacher.

1.	2.	3.	4.	5.

B How many?

C Fill in the missing numbers.

1. 10, ___, ___, 40, 50, ___, ___, 80.

2. 30, 40, ___, ___, ___, 80, 90, ___.

3. 100, ___, ___, 70, 60, ___, 40, ___.

Objectives: Explore, identify and record place value 0–99.

Strand	Number
Strand Unit	Addition

I will learn number patterns by counting.

A How many?

1. How many balloons?

2. Count the toes. How many are there?

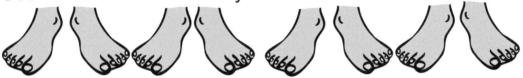

3. How many children in the line?

4. How many spots on all the ladybirds?

5. How many biscuits altogether?

6. Count the fingers. How many are there?

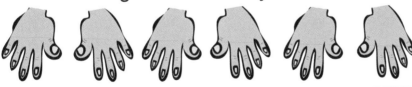

C Fill in the missing numbers.

2, ☐, ☐, 8, 10, ☐, ☐, 16, ☐, 20.

5, ☐, ☐, ☐, 25, ☐, ☐, 40, ☐, 50.

10, 20, ☐, ☐, ☐, 60, 70, ☐, ☐, 100.

Objectives: Explore and discuss repeated addition and group counting.

Strand Number
Strand Unit Addition

I will know $\frac{1}{2}$ of sets to 10.

A Do you remember your doubles?

1. $3 + 3 = \boxed{}$ 2. $1 + 1 = \boxed{}$ 3. $4 + 4 = \boxed{}$

4. $2 + 2 = \boxed{}$ 5. $5 + 5 = \boxed{}$ 6. $6 + 6 = \boxed{}$

B Count then circle $\frac{1}{2}$.

1. $= \boxed{}$. Now circle $\frac{1}{2}$. I circled $\boxed{}$ apple.

2. $= \boxed{}$. Now circle $\frac{1}{2}$. I circled $\boxed{}$ pears.

3.  $= \boxed{}$. Now circle $\frac{1}{2}$. I circled $\boxed{}$ bananas.

4.  $= \boxed{}$. Now circle $\frac{1}{2}$. I circled $\boxed{}$ oranges.

C Halves

$\frac{1}{2}$ of 2 $= \boxed{}$

$\frac{1}{2}$ of 4 $= \boxed{}$

$\frac{1}{2}$ of 6 $= \boxed{}$

$\frac{1}{2}$ of 8 $= \boxed{}$

$\frac{1}{2}$ of 10 $= \boxed{}$

D Draw $\frac{1}{2}$ an apple.

E Draw $\frac{1}{2}$ a cake.

I will know ½ of sets to 20.

A Count and colour ½.

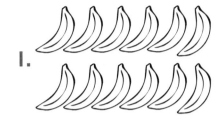

1. = ☐. Now colour ½. I coloured ☐ bananas.

2. = ☐. Now colour ½. I coloured ☐ oranges.

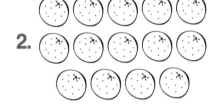

3. = ☐. Now colour ½. I coloured ☐ apples.

4. = ☐. Now colour ½. I coloured ☐ pears.

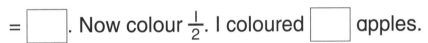

B Try these.

½ of 12 = ☐

½ of 14 = ☐

½ of 16 = ☐

½ of 18 = ☐

½ of 20 = ☐

C Kate's mum gave her **14** sweets to share with her sister, Molly. They each got ½ of the sweets . Draw the amount of sweets that Molly got.

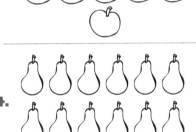

I will find ½ of 2D shapes.

A Match.

rectangle

square

circle

semi-circle

triangle

B Draw a line through each shape to show 2 halves. Colour.

Colour ▢   Colour ◖

Colour △   Colour ▭   Colour ●

C Tick the pizzas that show ½.

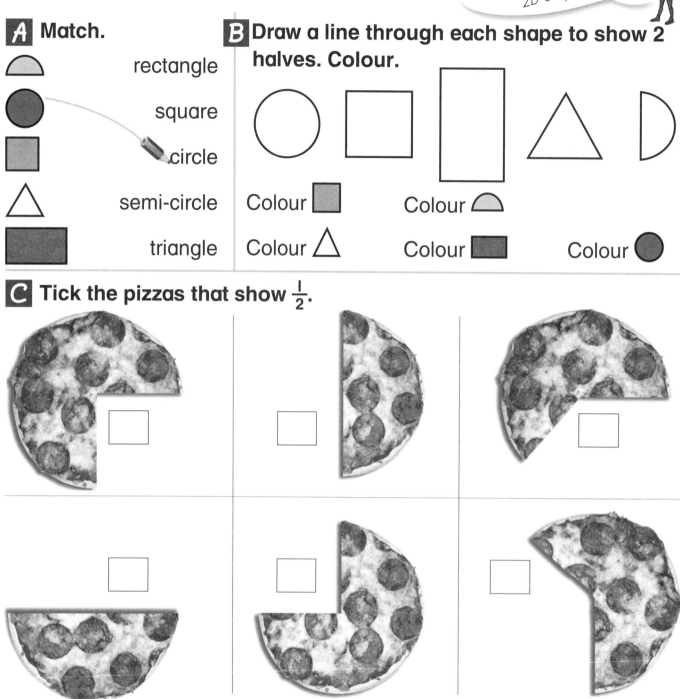

D *Pair work* Write the names of the shapes. Draw 2 lines on each shape to show halves in different ways.

 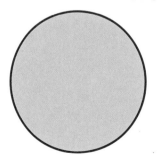 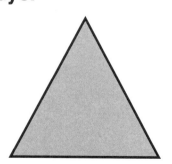

_____   _____   _____

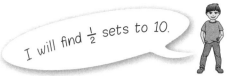

I will find ½ sets to 10.

A Tick the containers that are $\frac{1}{2}$ full.

B Tick the picture that show $\frac{1}{2}$.

C Colour $\frac{1}{2}$ of the chocolate bar.

Pair work

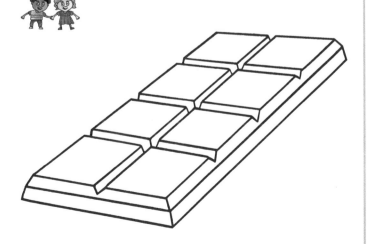

D Colour $\frac{1}{2}$ of the sweets.

Objectives Establish and identify half of sets to 20.

Strand   Number
Strand Unit   Fractions

Fractions

A *Pair work*  **Colour half.**

1.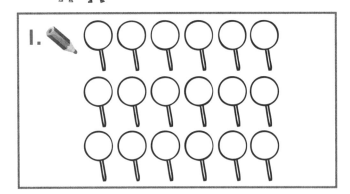

2.

3.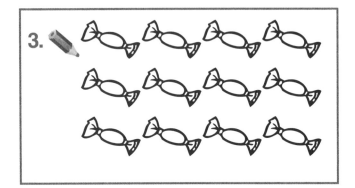

4.

B

1. John had **14** marbles. He gave $\frac{1}{2}$ to his friend Mark. How many did Mark get? ☐

2. Lisa had **6** cakes. She gave $\frac{1}{2}$ to Molly. How many cakes did Molly get? ☐

3. Mum gave Sarah and Tom $\frac{1}{2}$ a packet of sweets each. They each had **5** sweets. How many sweets were in the packet? ☐

4. Peter shared **20** cards into **two** equal piles. How many were in each pile? ☐

C **Match.**

$\frac{1}{2}$ of 12

$\frac{1}{2}$ of 16

$\frac{1}{2}$ of 20

$\frac{1}{2}$ of 18

$\frac{1}{2}$ of 14

8

7

6

9

10

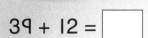

$39 + 12 = \boxed{}$

$39 + 10 + 2 = \boxed{51}$

I added the ten first and then the units.

1	2	3	4	5	6	7	8	9	10
11	12	13	14	15	16	17	18	19	20
21	22	23	24	25	26	27	28	29	30
31	32	33	34	35	36	37	38	39	40
41	42	43	44	45	46	47	48	49	50
51	52	53	54	55	56	57	58	59	60
61	62	63	64	65	66	67	68	69	70
71	72	73	74	75	76	77	78	79	80
81	82	83	84	85	86	87	88	89	90
91	92	93	94	95	96	97	98	99	100

A **Now try these. Use the 100 square.**

1. $44 + 10 = \boxed{}$ 2. $56 + 10 = \boxed{}$ 3. $75 + 10 = \boxed{}$

4. $27 + 20 = \boxed{}$ 5. $35 + 20 = \boxed{}$ 6. $55 + 20 = \boxed{}$

7. $33 + 30 = \boxed{}$ 8. $47 + 30 = \boxed{}$ 9. $61 + 30 = \boxed{}$

10. $23 + 40 = \boxed{}$ 11. $32 + 40 = \boxed{}$ 12. $12 + 40 = \boxed{}$

13. $14 + 40 = \boxed{}$ 14. $27 + 40 = \boxed{}$ 15. $55 + 40 = \boxed{}$

B **Try these.**

1. $28 + 31 = \boxed{}$ 2. $32 + 33 = \boxed{}$ 3. $22 + 15 = \boxed{}$

4. $14 + 41 = \boxed{}$ 5. $18 + 41 = \boxed{}$ 6. $35 + 21 = \boxed{}$

7. $28 + 41 = \boxed{}$ 8. $31 + 43 = \boxed{}$ 9. $33 + 36 = \boxed{}$

10. $42 + 45 = \boxed{}$ 11. $53 + 45 = \boxed{}$ 12. $75 + 14 = \boxed{}$

Objectives   Add numbers without renaming within 99.

Strand	Number
Strand Unit	Addition

Substraction

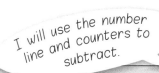

I will use the number line and counters to subtract.

A Warm-up. Listen to your teacher.

0 1 2 3 4 5 6 7 8 9 10 11 12 13 14 15 16 17 18 19 20

B

1. Mouse is on **15**. He jumped back **6** spaces. Where did he land?

   15 – 6 = ☐

   15
   – 6
   ___

2. Mouse is on **13**. He jumped back **5** spaces. Where did he land?

   13 – 5 = ☐

   13
   – 5
   ___

3. Mouse is on **17**. He jumped back **9** spaces. Where did he land?

   17 – 9 = ☐

   17
   – 9
   ___

4. Mouse is on **16**. He jumped back **7** spaces. Where did he land?

   16 – 7 = ☐

   16
   – 7
   ___

5. Mouse is on **18**. He jumped back **9** spaces. Where did he land?

   18 – 9 = ☐

   18
   – 9
   ___

C Try these. Use counters.

1. 18 – 6 = ☐

2. 17 – 8 = ☐

3. 19 – 9 = ☐

4. 15 – 7 = ☐

5. 14 – 8 = ☐

D Puzzle: Match. Colour.

10

9

7

8

6

12 – 6

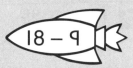
14 – 7

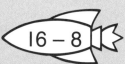
18 – 9

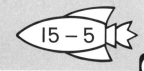
16 – 8

15 – 5

Objectives
• Construct number sentences and number stories.
• Solve problems involving subtraction 0–20.

Strand	Number
Strand Unit	Addition

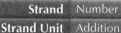

I will name, describe and compare 3D shapes.

A Warm-up. Listen to your teacher.

B Count.

cubes	cuboids	spheres	cylinders

C What rolls? Guess first. Then try.

shape	guess	✓ or ✗
cube		
cuboid		
sphere		
cylinder		

D Tick the shape that you think this makes:

cuboid ☐

sphere ☐

cylinder ☐

cube ☐

3D Shapes

A Count the 3D shapes in the picture.

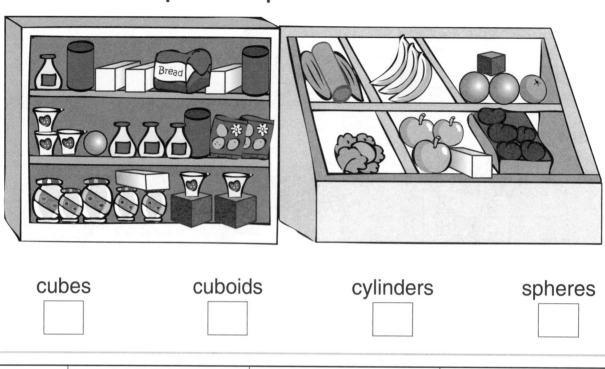

cubes

cuboids

cylinders

spheres

B

	How many faces?	How many edges?	How many corners?

C True or false? ✓ or X.

A sphere has 3 flat faces.

A sphere has I curved face.

A cube has 6 flat faces.

A cube has I0 edges.

A cylinder has 2 flat faces.

A cylinder has no corners.

A cuboid has I curved face.

A cuboid has 6 faces.

A Join the dots and write the name of each shape.

_____   _____   _____   _____

B Write the name beside each 3D shape.

cube   cylinder   sphere   cuboid

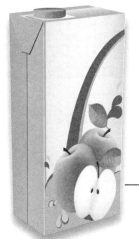

_____

_____

_____

_____

C Match.

cube

cylinder

sphere

cuboid

D Puzzle: If I put 2 cubes side by side, what 3D shapes would I make?

   _____

E In your copy, make a list of 5 3D shapes in your kitchen. Draw them.

3D Shapes

I will label sphere, cylinder, cuboid and cube.

A Write the names of the shapes.

_____ _____ _____ _____ _____

B Match – make the link!

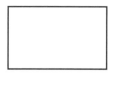 

C Count the cuboids.

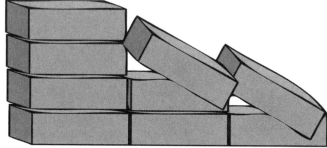

D How many dots on a dice? *Pair work*

E Look carefully at the 3D shapes. Can you spot any 2D shapes?

Colour: red blue ⬜ yellow *Groupwork*

cylinder	cube	cuboid
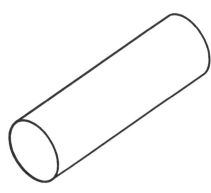	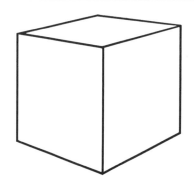	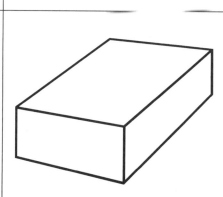

A I.

23
+ 14
[ ]

2. Colour half of the balls.

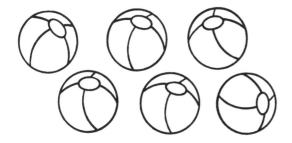

3. Circle the name of this shape.

triangle   square   semi-circle

4. Fill in the missing number.

46   47   48   49   [ ]

5. 14 + 0 = [ ]

6. 20, 30, [ ], [ ], 60, 70.

7. How many months in a season?   [ ]

8. Circle the one that holds the most.

   **8**

B I. Tick the **longest** snake.

[ ]
[ ]
[ ]

2. 20 – [ ] = 15

3. How many minutes in half an hour?

15 [ ]   30 [ ]   60 [ ]

4. Show 10 o'clock.

5. ✓ the lighter one.

[ ]   [ ]

6. How many faces on the cube?

   [ ]

7. How much for a and a ?   [ ] c

8. Show 45 on the abacus.

T   U

   **8**

Tables

Remember: When you add O to a number the number does not change.

1 + O = 1   3 + O = 3   7 + O = 7   O + 5 = 5   O + 9 = 9

A Add. Watch for the O.

2	+	O	=	
6	+	O	=	
7	+	9	=	
3	+	11	=	
8	+	9	=	
9	+	7	=	
10	+	8	=	
12	+	9	=	
9	+	5	=	
12	+	O	=	

B Add. Watch for the O.

O	+	9	=	
4	+	8	=	
14	+	2	=	
9	+	11	=	
6	+	8	=	
O	+	18	=	
5	+	14	=	
19	+	1	=	
11	+	7	=	
17	+	O	=	

C Now try some bigger numbers.

20	+	O	=	
24	+	O	=	
25	+	O	=	
27	+	O	=	
20	+	O	=	
27	+	O	=	
28	+	O	=	
26	+	O	=	
23	+	O	=	
29	+	O	=	

D Now try these.

O	+	66	=	
42	+	40	=	
80	+	21	=	
O	+	33	=	
71	+	7	=	
50	+	4	=	
O	+	76	=	
86	+	10	=	
O	+	92	=	
30	+	19	=	

Maths Trail

1 How many children in your class?

□

2 How many boys in your class?

□

3 How many girls in your class?

□

4 Are there more boys than girls in your class? Circle the correct answer.

yes   no

5 (a) How many windows in your classroom? □

(b) What shape are the windows? _____

6 (a) How many tables are in the room? □

(b) What shape are the top of the tables? _____

7 At what time do you start school?

_____

8 At what time do you leave school?

_____

9

colour key	
7	orange
9	green
4	yellow
6	blue
3	brown

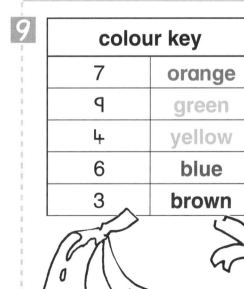
12 − 8
14 − 7

9

9 − 2

18 − 9

6 − 3

9 − 3

1. Alice is baking cookies. How many are on the tray? ☐

2. How many cookies on $\frac{1}{2}$ the tray? ☐

3. How many cookies could Alice make with **2** trays? ☐

4. The cookies will be ready at **3 o'clock**. Draw the hands on the clock.

5. How much milk does this bottle hold?

$\frac{1}{2}$ l ☐   1 l ☐   4 l ☐

6. Tick the one that is heavier.

 ☐    ☐

8. Look at the fridge below.
True or false? ✓ or ✗.

The oranges are **beside** the bread. ☐

The bread is **above** the eggs ☐

The bread is **below** the lettuce. ☐

The eggs are **left** of the butter. ☐

The bread is **below** the meat. ☐

7. Circle the foods that are good for you green.

Addition and Subtraction

If I know how to add, it's easy to subtract.

A How many altogether?

1.

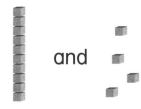 and

10 + 4 = ☐

4 + 10 = ☐

14 − 4 = ☐

14 − 10 = ☐

2.

 and

5 + 3 = ☐

3 + 5 = ☐

8 − 5 = ☐

8 − 3 = ☐

3.

 and

4 + 1 = ☐

1 + 4 = ☐

5 − 4 = ☐

5 − 1 = ☐

B Now try these. Use the numbers in the rectangles.

1.

| 13 |
| 10   3 |

☐ + ☐ = 13

☐ + ☐ = 13

☐ − ☐ = 10

☐ − ☐ = 3

2.

| 16 |
| 9   7 |

☐ + ☐ = ☐

☐ + ☐ = ☐

☐ − ☐ = ☐

☐ − ☐ = ☐

C Try these.

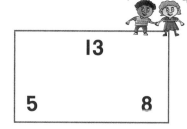

Pair work

1.

| 15 |
| 6   9 |

6 + 9 = ☐

9 + 6 = ☐

15 − ☐ = 6

15 − ☐ = 9

2.

| 17 |
| 10   7 |

10 + ☐ = 17

7 + ☐ = 17

17 − ☐ = 10

17 − ☐ = 7

3.

| 13 |
| 5   8 |

5 + ☐ = 13

8 + ☐ = 13

13 − ☐ = 8

13 − ☐ = 5

Objectives
- Focus on subtraction as the reverse of addition.
- Constructing number sentences.
- Develop recal strategies for addition and subtraction.

| Strand | Number |
| Strand Unit | Subtraction |

A Circle the numbers that are less than 10.

10   12   3   11   7   9   20

Circle the numbers that are more than 10.

2   9   11   15   20   5

B 0 1 2 3 4 5 6 7 8 9 10 11 12 13 14 15 16 17 18 19 20

Write the number that is:

1. 3 less than 20 ☐

2. 7 less than 12 ☐

3. 6 less than 14 ☐

4. 4 less than 10 ☐

5. 5 more than 8 ☐

6. 3 more than 9 ☐

7. 2 more than 9 ☐

8. 2 more than 8 ☐

9. 6 more than 10 ☐

10. 5 less than 8 ☐

C Try these.

1. Tara has **7** green apples. She also has **3** red apples. How many more green apples than red apples has she? ☐

2. Sean has **12** plums. Mary has **7** plums. How many more plums has Sean than Mary? ☐

3. Ann has **20c**. Tom has **14c**. How much more money has Ann than Tom? ☐ c

4. Ben has **12** pencils. Nora has **5** pencils. How many more pencils has Ben than Nora? ☐

D Puzzle: Which 2 zebras are the same? X them.

Strand	Number
Strand Unit	Subtraction

Subtraction

I will draw or use an abacus to subtract big numbers.

T U		T U	

Mary had 46 marbles

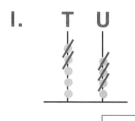

She lost 25 marbles. She had 21 left.

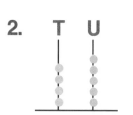

$46 - 25 = \boxed{21}$

$$\begin{array}{r} 46 \\ -25 \\ \hline 21 \end{array}$$

A Now try these.

1.   T U

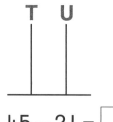

$54 - 23 = \boxed{31}$

2.   T U

$45 - 33 = \boxed{}$

3.   T U

$64 - 12 = \boxed{}$

4.   T U

$62 - 21 = \boxed{}$

B Now you can draw them.

T U

$45 - 21 = \boxed{}$

T U

$54 - 14 = \boxed{}$

T U

$65 - 34 = \boxed{}$

T U

$76 - 34 = \boxed{}$

C Now do these. Use an abacus if you need it.

1. T U	2. T U	3. T U	4. T U	5. T U	6. T U
4 9	6 7	8 5	9 6	7 8	5 7
− 2 3	− 3 5	− 4 3	− 2 3	− 1 8	− 4 6

7. T U	8. T U	9. T U	10. T U	11. T U	12. T U
8 7	5 9	7 8	6 5	9 8	4 9
− 3 5	− 2 7	− 6 3	− 3 4	− 6 2	− 1 7

Strand	Number
Strand Unit	Subtraction

I will learn about o'clock.

Time

133

A Warm-up. Listen to your teacher.

   24 12

B Write the time for each clock.

 | | |

4 o'clock | ___ o'clock | ___ o'clock | ___ o'clock

 | | |

___ o'clock | ___ o'clock | ___ o'clock | ___ o'clock

C Draw the hands on the clock.

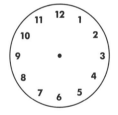 | 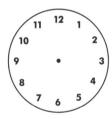 | 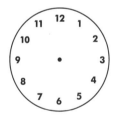 |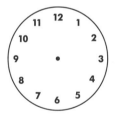

5 o'clock | 11 o'clock | 9 o'clock | 10 o'clock

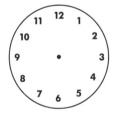 | 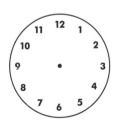 | 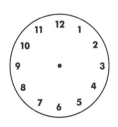 |

7 o'clock | 2 o'clock | 4 o'clock | 12 o'clock

D Write the missing numbers on the clocks.

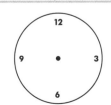 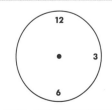 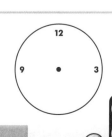

Objectives   Read the time in hours on a 12 hour analogue clock.

| Strand | Measures |
| Strand Unit | Time |

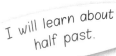

134 Time

I will learn about half past.

A Write the time.

half past 9

half past ☐

half past ☐

half past ☐

half past ☐

half past ☐

half past ☐

half past ☐

B Draw the hands on the clock.

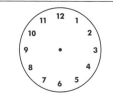

half past 2

half past 5

half past 3

half past 1

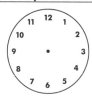

half past 8

half past 11

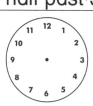

half past 12

half past 6

C Draw the picture and fill in the time.

I played football at half past 5.

I went to bed at half past 8.

Objectives Read the time in half hours on a 12 hour analogue clock.

Strand	Measures
Strand Unit	Time

I will learn about the months of the year.

A Months

1. How many months in a year? ☐
2. What is the third month? _____
3. The seventh month is _____.
4. Christmas Day is in _____.
5. Hallowe'en is in _____.
6. My birthday is in_____.

B Seasons

Pair work

1. How many seasons are there? ☐
2. Summer comes after _____.
3. Summer comes before _____.
4. How many months in a season? ☐
5. St Patrick's Day is in _____.
6. The warmest season is _____.

C Draw your favourite season.

winter	January
spring	February
	March
	April
summer	May
	June
	July
autumn	August
	September
	October
winter	November
	December 

I will learn how to read a calendar.

A Fill in the missing numbers on the calendar.

MARCH						
Monday	Tuesday	Wednesday	Thursday	Friday	Saturday	Sunday
		1		3	4	5
6		8	9		11	
13	14		16		18	19
	21		23		25	26
27		29		31		

1. How many days in March? ☐

2. How many Sundays in March? ☐

3. How many Saturdays in March? ☐

4. What day is the seventh of March? _____

5. What day is the ninth of March? _____

6. What day is the second Wednesday of March? _____

B

1. Tara came to school at _____ o'clock.
2. Tara played at _____ o'clock.
3. Tara had dinner at _____ o'clock.
4. Tara was asleep at _____ o'clock.

Strand	Measures
Strand Unit	Time

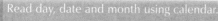

2 tens + ①l units = ⦙3⦙ tens + ⦙ ⦙ unit

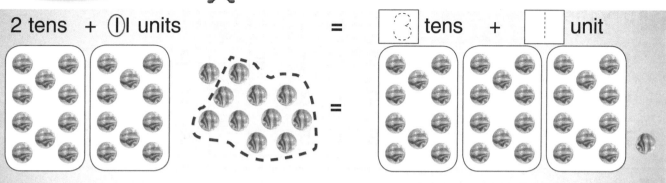

A Add

1. 4 tens + 13 units = ☐ tens + ☐ units

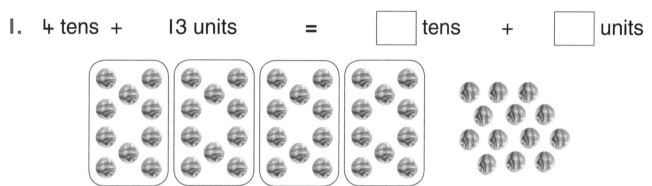

2. 5 tens + 11 units = ☐ tens + ☐ unit

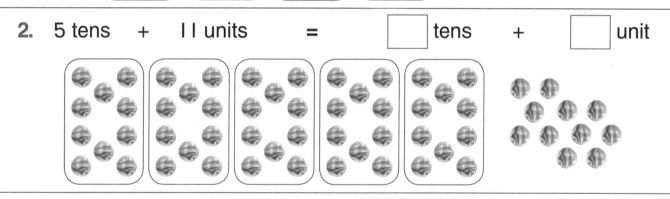

3. 6 tens + 15 units = ☐ tens + ☐ units

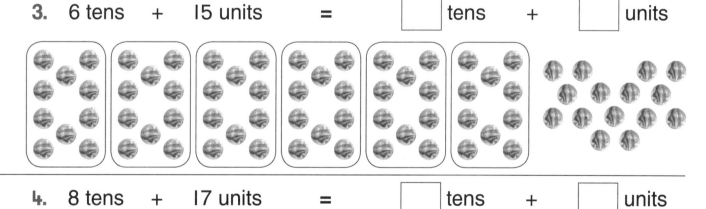

4. 8 tens + 17 units = ☐ tens + ☐ units

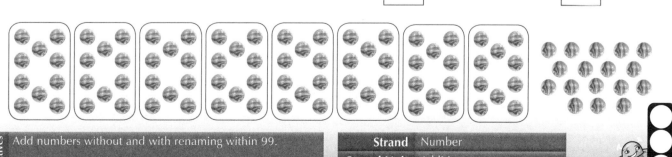

A Try these.

1. 7 + 3 = ☐   2. 5 + 1 = ☐   3. 9 + 2 = ☐
4. 7 + 4 = ☐   5. 9 + 8 = ☐   6. 2 + 9 = ☐
7. 8 + 0 = ☐   8. 3 + 5 = ☐   9. 8 + 7 = ☐

B Fill in the number.

1. 2 tens + ⓪5 units = | 3 | tens + | 5 | units
2. 3 tens + 17 units = ☐ tens + ☐ units
3. 6 tens + 11 units = ☐ tens + ☐ unit
4. 4 tens + 16 units = ☐ tens + ☐ units
5. 2 tens + 19 units = ☐ tens + ☐ units
6. 6 tens + 12 units = ☐ tens + ☐ units
7. 7 tens + 14 units = ☐ tens + ☐ units
8. 8 tens + 13 units = ☐ tens + ☐ units
9. 5 tens + 11 units = ☐ tens + ☐ unit
10. 8 tens + 18 units = ☐ tens + ☐ units
11. 3 tens + 15 units = ☐ tens + ☐ units
12. 6 tens + 10 units = ☐ tens + ☐ units

C Match.

4 tens + 15 units ——— 65
2 tens + 13 units   55
5 tens + 15 units   81
7 tens + 11 units   94
8 tens + 14 units   33

6 tens + 12 units 51
3 tens + 17 units   36
5 tens + 10 units   72
4 tens + 11 units   47
2 tens + 16 units   60

A Try these.

1. 8 + 8 = ☐   2. 9 + 7 = ☐   3. 9 + 6 = ☐

4. 8 + 4 = ☐   5. 8 + 3 = ☐   6. 9 + 9 = ☐

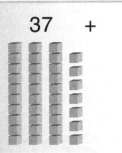

| 37 | + | 15 |

```
     3 tens  +   7 units
  +  1 ten   +   5 units
  ─────────────────────────
     4 tens  +  12 units
  =  5 tens  +   2 units
```

B Fill in the missing numbers.

1.
```
    2 tens  +  5 units
 +  2 tens  +  9 units
 ─────────────────────
   ☐ tens   ☐ units
```

2.
```
    4 tens  +  3 units
 +  1 ten   +  8 units
 ─────────────────────
   ☐ tens   ☐ units
```

3.
```
    3 tens  +  8 units
 +  2 tens  +  8 units
 ─────────────────────
   ☐ tens   ☐ units
```

4.
```
    3 tens  +  9 units
 +  4 tens  +  6 units
 ─────────────────────
   ☐ tens   ☐ units
```

5.
```
    4 tens  +  9 units
 +  4 tens  +  8 units
 ─────────────────────
   ☐ tens   ☐ units
```

6.
```
    4 tens  +  9 units
 +  3 tens  +  9 units
 ─────────────────────
   ☐ tens   ☐ units
```

7.
```
    3 tens  +  5 units
 +  3 tens  +  7 units
 ─────────────────────
   ☐ tens   ☐ units
```

8.
```
    5 tens  +  7 units
 +  1 ten   +  7 units
 ─────────────────────
   ☐ tens   ☐ units
```

A Circle the tens.

⑴3   16   29   24   33   41   74

Circle the units.

1⑴   20   37   45   51   62   86

B Try these.

1. tens units	2. tens units	3. tens units
3 5	3 4	3 7
+ 2₁ 7	+ 3 8	+ 4 7

4. tens units	5. tens units	6. tens units
4 8	6 9	7 9
+ 2 8	+ 2 3	+ 1 6

7. tens units	8. tens units	9. tens units
2 9	5 6	3 7
+ 4 9	+ 2 6	+ 4 3

C Use cubes to help you.

1.   2 tens + 8 units
+ 1₁ tens + 3 units
    [4] tens [1] unit

2.   3 tens + 7 units
+   2 tens + 5 units
    [ ] tens [ ] units

3.   5 tens + 4 units
+   2 tens + 9 units
    [ ] tens [ ] units

4.   5 tens + 8 units
+   3 tens + 7 units
    [ ] tens [ ] units

Objectives: Add numbers without and with renaming within 99.

Strand Number
Strand Unit Addition

A Add.

1. (a) 18
   + 26

   (b) 28
   + 19

   (c) 36
   + 26

   (d) 55
   + 19

   (e) 28
   + 28

2. (a) 37
   + 14

   (b) 28
   + 35

   (c) 25
   + 39

   (d) 18
   + 63

   (e) 33
   + 49

3. (a) 22
   + 49

   (b) 35
   + 57

   (c) 19
   + 65

   (d) 38
   + 52

4. (a) 47
   + 29

   (b) 37
   + 59

   (c) 19
   + 43

   (d) 15
   + 69

   (e) 29
   + 39

B Try these.

1. Susan has **11** books. John has **8** books. How many books have Susan and John?

2. William spent **12c** in the shop. James spent **5c** in the shop. How much money did they both spend altogether? [ ]c

3. Amy has **9** sweets. Dermot has **9** sweets. How many sweets have Amy and Dermot?

4. Sean has **7** marbles. Elaine has **8** more. How many has Elaine?

5. Simon has **13c**. Lisa has **5c** more than Simon. How much money has Lisa? [ ]c

Addition

A Circle the tens.

12   14   27   38   42   53   55

Circle the units.

24   33   42   58   41   34   44

B Try these.

1.	tens	units	2.	tens	units	3.	tens	units	4.	tens	units
	2	6		1	4		2	8		3	5
+	1₁	6	+	3	9	+	3	6	+	1	8
	4	2									

5.	tens	units	6.	tens	units	7.	tens	units	8.	tens	units
	6	2		2	7		5	6		4	8
+	2	9	+	3	7	+	2	7	+	2	9

C Try these.

1. 47 + 29 = ☐   2. 28 + 63 = ☐

3. 55 + 28 = ☐   4. 47 + 24 = ☐

5. 11 + 59 = ☐   6. 35 + 19 = ☐

7. 33 + 28 = ☐   8. 55 + 38 = ☐

9. 58 + 18 = ☐   10. 17 + 58 = ☐

11. 26 + 36 = ☐   12. 33 + 27 = ☐

D

1. Sam had **15c**. Tony gave him another **18c**. How much has Sam now? ☐ c

2. There were **15** lollipops in a jar. Alex added **17** more. How many lollipops in the jar now? ☐

Strand	Number
Strand Unit	Addition

A 1. 25, 35, 45, 55, ☐ , 75

2. ✗ the square.

3. What time is one hour after 12 o'clock? _____

4. How much? ☐ c

5. 26
    + 16
    ☐

6. How many animals altogether? ☐

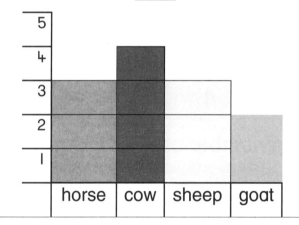

	5			
	4			
	3			
	2			
	1			
	horse	cow	sheep	goat

7. 3 + 4 = 4 + ☐

8. How much was eaten?

$\frac{1}{2}$ ☐   less than $\frac{1}{2}$ ☐

8

B 1.

June						
S	M	T	W	T	F	S
	1	2	3	4	5	6
7	8	9	10	11	12	13
14	15	16	17	18	19	20
21	22	23	24	25	26	27
28	29	30				

How many Mondays? ☐

2. 8 + 3 + 2 = ☐

3. Tick the number shown on the abacus.

T   U

22 ☐

42 ☐

24 ☐

4. Finish the pattern.

5.

64
+ 23
☐

6. 7 – ☐ = 5

7. Show 2 o'clock.

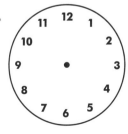

8. 12 + ☐ = 15

8

Tables

Subtraction

When you subtract you move backwards.

e.g. 7 – 2 = 5

Cover 7 with a counter, then use your finger to count 2 spaces backwards. Where did you land? Yes you landed on 5.

1	2	3	4	5	6	7	8	9	10
11	12	13	14	15	16	17	18	19	20
21	22	23	24	25	26	27	28	29	30
31	32	33	34	35	36	37	38	39	40
41	42	43	44	45	46	47	48	49	50
51	52	53	54	55	56	57	58	59	60
61	62	63	64	65	66	67	68	69	70
71	72	73	74	75	76	77	78	79	80
81	82	83	84	85	86	87	88	89	90
91	92	93	94	95	96	97	98	99	100

A **Use a counter to cover your starting number on the 100 grid. Practise counting backwards.**

1. $12 - 2 =$ ☐ $13 - 2 =$ ☐ $32 - 2 =$ ☐

2. $23 - 4 =$ ☐ $23 - 4 -$ ☐ $43 - 4 -$ ☐

3. $35 - 3 =$ ☐ $55 - 3 =$ ☐ $85 - 3 =$ ☐

B 1. $72 - 6 =$ ☐ $43 - 4 =$ ☐ $38 - 5 =$ ☐ $61 - 2 =$ ☐

2. $85 - 5 =$ ☐ $93 - 2 =$ ☐ $49 - 7 =$ ☐ $48 - 6 =$ ☐

3. $96 - 6 =$ ☐ $88 - 7 =$ ☐ $67 - 5 =$ ☐ $78 - 8 =$ ☐

1 All the children's ages relate to their names. Can you work out how old Thomas is?

Harry is 5. Martin is 6. Caroline is 8. Josephine is 9. Thomas is ☐.

2

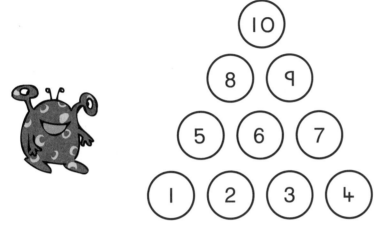

Take 10 coins or buttons and arrange them like the ones above.

Can you move only three coins to make the triangle turn upside down?

3 Which of these numbers is the odd one out? Colour the odd one out and explain why.

| 1. | 2 | 4 | 5 | 8 | 10 |

| 2. | 12 | 10 | 8 | 5 |

| 3. | 29 | 28 | 27 | 22 |

| 4. | 20 | 30 | 40 | 35 |

| 5. | 1 | 3 | 5 | 7 | 8 |

| 6. | 92 | 82 | 70 | 62 |

4 **Break the code.**

What are the alien's favourite foods?

1. 50 − 20 = _____ (P)   2.   8 + 4 = _____ (I)
3. 20 − 6 = _____ (Z)   4. 20 − 5 = _____ (L)
5. 10 + 11 = _____ (C)   6. 20 − 2 = _____ (A)
7. 10 − 7 = _____ (O)   8. 15 + 5 = _____ (T)
9. 20 − 12 = _____ (R)   10. 10 − 5 = _____ (S)
11. $\frac{1}{2}$ of 14 = _____ (E)

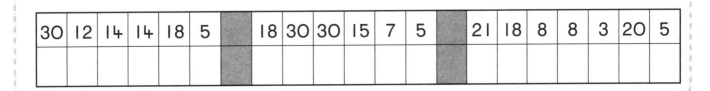

30	12	14	14	18	5		18	30	30	15	7	5		21	18	8	8	3	20	5

You will need a dice and a counter for each player.

Green means go forward.

Red means go back.

Fill in the missing numbers as you play.

Do you know the story
of the enormous turnip?

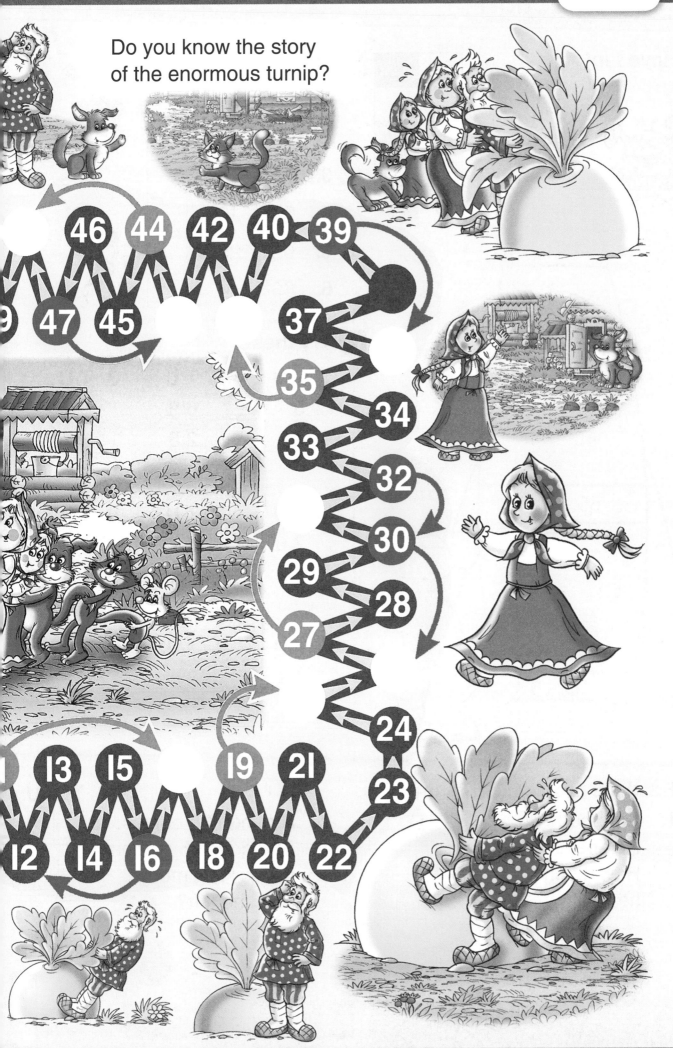

Subtraction

I will practise subtraction sums.

A Have fun!

2	
3	
4	
5	
6	

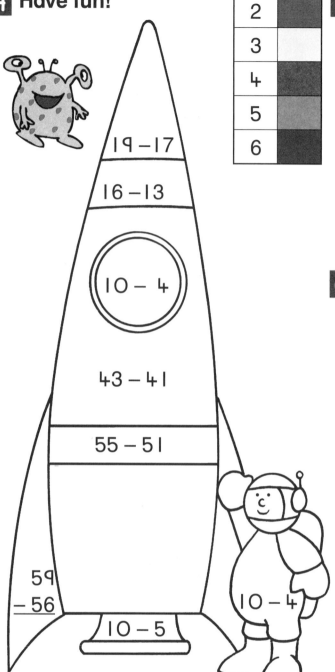

19 − 17

16 − 13

10 − 4

43 − 41

55 − 51

59 − 56

10 − 5

10 − 4

B Use cubes or beads.

1. 28 − 15 = ☐
2. 49 − 16 = ☐
3. 78 − 14 = ☐
4. 57 − 16 = ☐
5. 69 − 25 = ☐
6. 86 − 14 = ☐

C Try these.

1. T U	2. T U	3. T U
5 7	6 9	8 7
− 1 4	− 2 5	− 3 7

4. T U	5. T U	6. T U
7 6	8 7	6 7
− 3 2	− 2 5	− 1 7

7. T U	8. T U	9. T U
8 4	9 7	7 9
− 2 4	− 3 4	− 3 6

D Read the problem. Write the sum.

1. Sam had **76c.** He spent **43c.** How much had he left?

   T U
   ☐ ☐
   − ☐ ☐
   ☐ ☐

2. Ann had **38** apples. She gave **25** of them away. How many had she left?

   T U
   ☐ ☐
   − ☐ ☐
   ☐ ☐

Objectives — Subtract numbers without renaming within 99.

Strand	Number
Strand Unit	Subtraction

I will look for an easy way to subtract big numbers.

A Try these.

1. $45 - 10 = \boxed{}$ 2. $56 - 10 = \boxed{}$ 3. $76 - 20 = \boxed{}$

$39 - 12$

$39 - 12 = \boxed{?}$

$39 - 12$ is the same as $(39 - 10) - 2 = 27$

I subtracted the ten first and then the units.

B Now try these. Use the 100 square if you wish.

1. $32 - 12 = \boxed{}$ 2. $28 - 11 = \boxed{}$ 3. $73 - 11 = \boxed{}$

4. $49 - 13 = \boxed{}$ 5. $58 - 14 = \boxed{}$ 6. $69 - 15 = \boxed{}$

7. $78 - 21 = \boxed{}$ 8. $58 - 22 = \boxed{}$ 9. $97 - 25 = \boxed{}$

10. $77 - 25 = \boxed{}$ 11. $66 - 32 = \boxed{}$ 12. $68 - 23 = \boxed{}$

13. $48 - 31 = \boxed{}$ 14. $79 - 33 = \boxed{}$ 15. $66 - 35 = \boxed{}$

C Try these. Use an abacus or the 100 square if you wish.

1. $89 - 32 = \boxed{}$ 2. $95 - 31 = \boxed{}$

3. $77 - 42 = \boxed{}$ 4. $87 - 43 = \boxed{}$

5. $98 - 45 = \boxed{}$ 6. $79 - 46 = \boxed{}$

7. $99 - 46 = \boxed{}$ 8. $89 - 42 = \boxed{}$

D Try these.

1. $\begin{array}{r} 77 \\ -51 \\ \hline \end{array}$ 2. $\begin{array}{r} 69 \\ -34 \\ \hline \end{array}$ 3. $\begin{array}{r} 87 \\ -53 \\ \hline \end{array}$ 4. $\begin{array}{r} 68 \\ -25 \\ \hline \end{array}$

5. $\begin{array}{r} 84 \\ -30 \\ \hline \end{array}$ 6. $\begin{array}{r} 76 \\ -46 \\ \hline \end{array}$ 7. $\begin{array}{r} 39 \\ -15 \\ \hline \end{array}$ 8. $\begin{array}{r} 57 \\ -40 \\ \hline \end{array}$

Subtraction

I will learn to subtract big numbers.

Tom had 77 cubes

He gave 34 to Tara. He had 43 left.

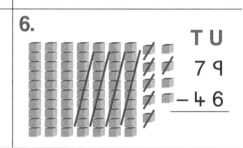

```
   7 7
 - 3 4
   4 3
```

A Now try these.

1.
```
   T U
   3 5
 - 2 4
```

2.
```
   T U
   4 7
 - 1 2
```

3.
```
   T U
   8 6
 - 3 6
```

4.
```
   T U
   5 4
 - 3 3
```

5.
```
   T U
   6 8
 - 5 5
```

6.
```
   T U
   7 9
 - 4 6
```

B Use cubes or beads to do these.

1.
```
 T U
 3 6
-2 4
```

2.
```
 T U
 4 7
-2 7
```

3.
```
 T U
 5 8
-3 2
```

4.
```
 T U
 6 9
-2 4
```

5.
```
 T U
 7 5
-3 5
```

6.
```
 T U
 9 5
-4 3
```

7.
```
 T U
 8 6
-2 3
```

8.
```
 T U
 7 7
-2 4
```

9.
```
 T U
 8 7
-3 1
```

10.
```
 T U
 4 6
-1 6
```

C

1. Rose had **27c**. She spent **15c**. How much had she left? ▢ c

2. Pat had **36** marbles. He lost **24** of them. How many had he left? ▢

3. Tara had **59** cards. She gave away **25** of them. How many had she left? ▢

I will use coins up to the value of 50c.

Money   151

A What is the value of the missing coins?

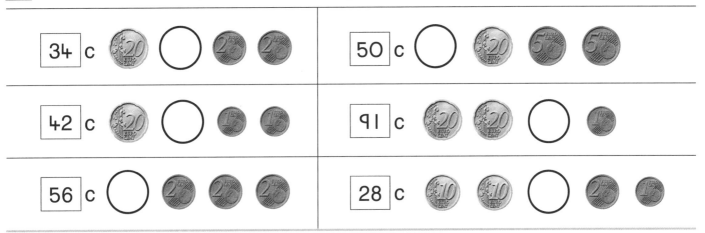

B What is the cost of the shopping in the bags below?

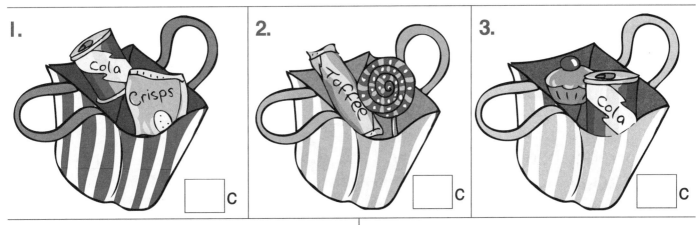

1.   2.   3.

☐ c   ☐ c   ☐ c

4.   5.

☐ c   ☐ c

Objectives
- Recognise, exchange and use coins up to the value of 50c.
- Calculate how many items may be bought with a given sum.

Strand	Measures
Strand Unit	Money

Money

I will use coins up to the value of 50c.

A How much change do I get?

 8c  27c   10c  7c   9c

I have	I buy	cost	my change
25c			
15c			
35c			
42c			
46c			
28c			

B How many?

1. How many ice-cream cones can I buy with **20c**? ▢

   How much change? ▢ c

2. How many bananas can I buy with **30c**? ▢

   How much change? ▢ c

3. How many loaves of bread can I buy with **50c**? ▢

   How much change? ▢ c

C Fill in the missing coins.

1.
 = 10c

2.
 = 20c

3.
 = 50c

4.
 = 12c

Objectives Calculate how many items may be bought with a given sum.

Strand	Measures
Strand Unit	Money

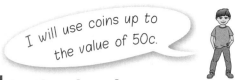

I will use coins up to the value of 50c.

A Let's shop!

1. How much is a  and a  ? ☐ c

2. How much is a 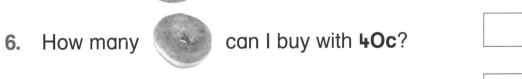 and a 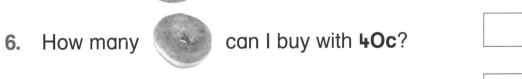 ? ☐ c

3. How much is a 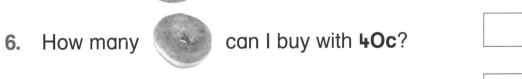 and a 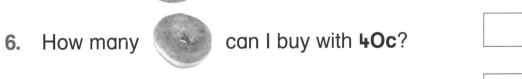 ? ☐ c

4. How many 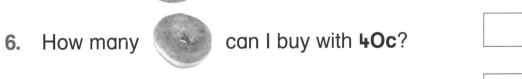 can I buy with **30c**? ☐

5. How many 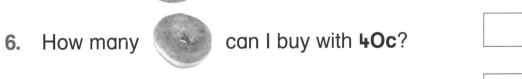 can I buy with **20c**? ☐

6. How many 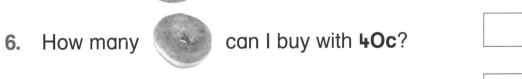 can I buy with **40c**? ☐

7. How many 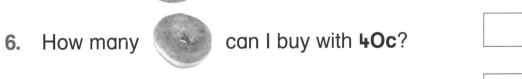 can I buy with **30c**? ☐

Strand	Measures
Strand Unit	Money

Money

I will use coins up to the value of 50c.

A **Find the cost of the shopping bags below.**

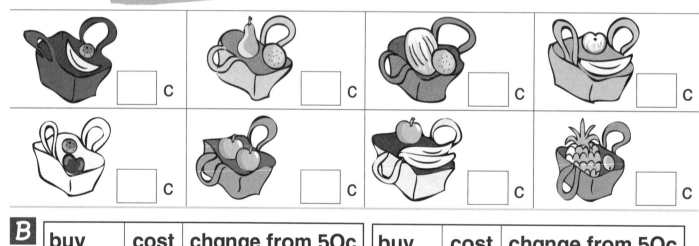

B

buy	cost	change from 50c	buy	cost	change from 50c

Strand	Measures
Strand Unit	Money

A 1. Colour half of this shape.

2. How many faces has a cube?

   4 ☐

   6 ☐

   8 ☐

3. $(6 + 3) + 1 = 6 + (3 + \boxed{})$

4. What comes next? Draw and colour.

 ☐

5. $45 - 23 = \boxed{}$

6. How much?

 ☐ c

7. $10 + 2 = \boxed{} + 3$

8. Which is heavier?

   pencil ☐

   bun ☐

$\boxed{8}$

B 1. Show half past 8.

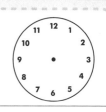

2. Does an egg cup hold more than ☐ or less than ☐ 1 litre?

3. $\begin{array}{r} 43 \\ -27 \\ \hline \end{array}$

4. Colour the coins for 8c.

5. $20 - \boxed{} = 11$

6. $\begin{array}{r} 56 \\ -24 \\ \hline \end{array}$

7. What day is the 12th?

   _____

August						
M	T	W	T	F	S	S
	1	2	3	4	5	6
7	8	9	10	11	12	13
14	15	16	17	18	19	20
21	22	23	24	25	26	27
28	29	30	31			

8. Show 53 on the abacus.

   T   U

$\boxed{8}$

A

1. cube ☐   sphere ☐   cylinder ☐

2.
$$19 + 65$$
☐

3. $18 - \boxed{} = 11$

4. $33 + 21 = \boxed{}$

5. Show half past 2 on the clock.

6. How much is an apple and an orange? Circle the correct answer.

 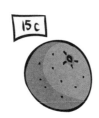

20c

27c

17c

7.
$$98 - 62$$
☐

8. There are ☐ more cats than dogs.

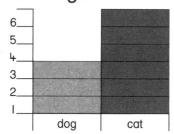

8

B

1. $15 - \boxed{} = 12$

2.    circle ☐   triangle ☐   square ☐

3. $8 + 3 + \boxed{} = 15$

4.
$$56 + 8$$
☐

5.

☐ tens ☐ units

6. How much?

     ☐ c

7. Who is tallest? _____

Barry   Jim   Molly

8.
$$65 - 34$$
☐

8

Symbols

+ means add   **—** means subtract   **=** means is the same as

Fractions

1 whole

2 halves

2D shapes

circle
1 side
0 corners

square
4 sides
4 corners

triangle
3 sides
3 corners

rectangle
4 sides
4 corners

3D shapes

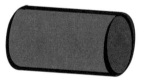

cylinder
3 faces
0 corners

sphere
1 face
0 corners

cuboid
6 faces
8 corners

cube
6 edges
8 corners

Measurements
Measure liquid

1 litre

$\frac{1}{2}$ litre

Time

When the big hand is on 12, it is o'clock.

When the big hand is on 6, it is half past.

Addition Tables

Remember:
2 + 3 is the same as
3 + 2

1 + 0 = 1	2 + 0 = 2	3 + 0 = 3
1 + 1 = 2	2 + 1 = 3	3 + 1 = 4
1 + 2 = 3	2 + 2 = 4	3 + 2 = 5
1 + 3 = 4	2 + 3 = 5	3 + 3 = 6
1 + 4 = 5	2 + 4 = 6	3 + 4 = 7
1 + 5 = 6	2 + 5 = 7	3 + 5 = 8
1 + 6 = 7	2 + 6 = 8	3 + 6 = 9
1 + 7 = 8	2 + 7 = 9	3 + 7 = 10
1 + 8 = 9	2 + 8 = 10	3 + 8 = 11
1 + 9 = 10	2 + 9 = 11	3 + 9 = 12
1 + 10 = 11	2 + 10 = 12	3 + 10 = 13

4 + 0 = 4	5 + 0 = 5	6 + 0 = 6	7 + 0 = 7
4 + 1 = 5	5 + 1 = 6	6 + 1 = 7	7 + 1 = 8
4 + 2 = 6	5 + 2 = 7	6 + 2 = 8	7 + 2 = 9
4 + 3 = 7	5 + 3 = 8	6 + 3 = 9	7 + 3 = 10
4 + 4 = 8	5 + 4 = 9	6 + 4 = 10	7 + 4 = 11
4 + 5 = 9	5 + 5 = 10	6 + 5 = 11	7 + 5 = 12
4 + 6 = 10	5 + 6 = 11	6 + 6 = 12	7 + 6 = 13
4 + 7 = 11	5 + 7 = 12	6 + 7 = 13	7 + 7 = 14
4 + 8 = 12	5 + 8 = 13	6 + 8 = 14	7 + 8 = 15
4 + 9 = 13	5 + 9 = 14	6 + 9 = 15	7 + 9 = 16
4 + 10 = 14	5 + 10 = 15	6 + 10 = 16	7 + 10 = 17

8 + 0 = 8	9 + 0 = 9	10 + 0 = 10
8 + 1 = 9	9 + 1 = 10	10 + 1 = 11
8 + 2 = 10	9 + 2 = 11	10 + 2 = 12
8 + 3 = 11	9 + 3 = 12	10 + 3 = 13
8 + 4 = 12	9 + 4 = 13	10 + 4 = 14
8 + 5 = 13	9 + 5 = 14	10 + 5 = 15
8 + 6 = 14	9 + 6 = 15	10 + 6 = 16
8 + 7 = 15	9 + 7 = 16	10 + 7 = 17
8 + 8 = 16	9 + 8 = 17	10 + 8 = 18
8 + 9 = 17	9 + 9 = 18	10 + 9 = 19
8 + 10 = 18	9 + 10 = 19	10 + 10 = 20

If you know the tables in green, you already know the rest.

1	−	1	=	0
2	−	1	=	1
3	−	1	=	2
4	−	1	=	3
5	−	1	=	4
6	−	1	=	5
7	−	1	=	6
8	−	1	=	7
9	−	1	=	8
10	−	1	=	9
11	−	1	=	10

2	−	2	=	0
3	−	2	=	1
4	−	2	=	2
5	−	2	=	3
6	−	2	=	4
7	−	2	=	5
8	−	2	=	6
9	−	2	=	7
10	−	2	=	8
11	−	2	=	9
12	−	2	=	10

3	−	3	=	0
4	−	3	=	1
5	−	3	=	2
6	−	3	=	3
7	−	3	=	4
8	−	3	=	5
9	−	3	=	6
10	−	3	=	7
11	−	3	=	8
12	−	3	=	9
13	−	3	=	10

If you know your addition tables, your substraction tables are easy.

4	−	4	=	0
5	−	4	=	1
6	−	4	=	2
7	−	4	=	3
8	−	4	=	4
9	−	4	=	5
10	−	4	=	6
11	−	4	=	7
12	−	4	=	8
13	−	4	=	9
14	−	4	=	10

5	−	5	=	0
6	−	5	=	1
7	−	5	=	2
8	−	5	=	3
9	−	5	=	4
10	−	5	=	5
11	−	5	=	6
12	−	5	=	7
13	−	5	=	8
14	−	5	=	9
15	−	5	=	10

6	−	6	=	0
7	−	6	=	1
8	−	6	=	2
9	−	6	=	3
10	−	6	=	4
11	−	6	=	5
12	−	6	=	6
13	−	6	=	7
14	−	6	=	8
15	−	6	=	9
16	−	6	=	10

7	−	7	=	0
8	−	7	=	1
9	−	7	=	2
10	−	7	=	3
11	−	7	=	4
12	−	7	=	5
13	−	7	=	6
14	−	7	=	7
15	−	7	=	8
16	−	7	=	9
17	−	7	=	10

Remember:
2 + 3 = 5
3 + 2 = 5
5 − 2 = 3
5 − 3 = 2

8	−	8	=	0
9	−	8	=	1
10	−	8	=	2
11	−	8	=	3
12	−	8	=	4
13	−	8	=	5
14	−	8	=	6
15	−	8	=	7
16	−	8	=	8
17	−	8	=	9
18	−	8	=	10

9	−	9	=	0
10	−	9	=	1
11	−	9	=	2
12	−	9	=	3
13	−	9	=	4
14	−	9	=	5
15	−	9	=	6
16	−	9	=	7
17	−	9	=	8
18	−	9	=	9
19	−	9	=	10

10	−	10	=	0
11	−	10	=	1
12	−	10	=	2
13	−	10	=	3
14	−	10	=	4
15	−	10	=	5
16	−	10	=	6
17	−	10	=	7
18	−	10	=	8
19	−	10	=	9
20	−	10	=	10

Colour by Number

Well done for finishing the book!